From Pieces to Peace

32 YEARS OF LESBIANISM

FINALLY LETTING GO OF THE CHAINS OF AN UNCLEAN SPIRIT

Tanya S. Meade

Tanya S. Meade

From Pieces to Peace

*32 Years of Lesbianism:
Finally Letting Go of the
Chains of an Unclean Spirit*

Foreword By:
Pastor Vernell Gabriel

Cover Design By:
Jacquelyn Foster, Eden Creative Designs
EdenCreativeDesigns@gmail.com

Pearly Gates Publishing LLC, Houston, Texas

From Pieces to Peace

From Pieces to Peace
32 Years of Lesbianism:
Finally Letting Go of the
Chains of an Unclean Spirit

Copyright © 2017
Tanya Meade

All Rights Reserved.
No portion of this publication may be reproduced, stored in any electronic system, or transmitted in any form or by any means (electronic, mechanical, photocopy, recording, or otherwise) without written permission from the author or publisher. Brief quotations may be used in literary reviews.

Some names and identifying details have been changed to protect the privacy of individuals.

ISBN 13: 978-1945117824
ISBN 10: 1945117826
Library of Congress Control Number: 2017946914

Scripture references are used with permission from Zondervan via Biblegateway.com.

For information and bulk ordering, contact:
Pearly Gates Publishing LLC
Angela R. Edwards
P.O. Box 62287
Houston, TX 77205
BestSeller@PearlyGatesPublishing.com

Tanya S. Meade

DEDICATION

This book is first and foremost dedicated to my Lord and Savior, Jesus Christ.

I then dedicate this book to my Spiritual Godmother, BFF, and Great Woman of God, **Pastor Vernell Gabriel**, and my other good friend, **Cathy**, who were praying for me the entire time since their own deliverance from that lifestyle.

I also dedicate this to God's people who are waiting for this book - including myself. Homosexuality was a stronghold I never thought I would be delivered from…**BUT GOD!**

From Pieces to Peace

ACKNOWLEDGEMENTS

First, giving honor to the Love of my soul: Jesus Christ. We call Him Yeshua HaMashiach, the Lord my God, and the Holy Spirit.

I also desire to acknowledge a few people who, in some way during my journey to freedom, impacted my life.

To my Spiritual Godmother, Pastor Vernell Gabriel: Thank you for being a pillar for me as I came out of the LBGTQ Church. You wanted so badly to say something to me, but God silenced you and didn't allow you to speak over me. He assured you He had me covered, and I am forever grateful for you.

To Cathy: You are another friend who was delivered some 30 years go. Thank you for being there with and for me.

I want to thank a few people whom God allowed me to meet through Periscope - those who encouraged me, spoke, and sowed seeds: **Prophet Marcus Rivers, Apostle Marc Mays, Prophetess Jolynne Whittaker, Apostle Marlo Dickson, Evangelist Raffael Gray, Prophet Norman Bryant, Prophet Scott Hood, Prophetess Sophia Ruffin, Kenyetta M. Hall, Rev. Tenko Kayzer, Apostles Will and Hannah, Prophet Shawndell Huggins, Erica Garcia, Tanya Nelson, Apostle Vails, Prophetess Andrea Harris,** and **Apostle Richard Youngblood.**

To a special group of people in my SDM class: **Prophet Charles Shelton, Jr., Prophetess Corazon GilesMendoza, Minister Shirley Williams, KiKi Jones, Minister Orencia Bulze, Natasha Joseph Deleon,** and **Kim Harrison.**

Tanya S. Meade

To my Sister Intercessors: **Prophetess Jonette Sheridan** and **Prophetess Autumn Sheridan.**

To my *Write Like A Pro* Family: **Minister Catherine Storing, Angela Edwards, Andrea Freygang,** and **Jacci Foster.**

Last, but not least, my family members: **Steven Foster, Aaron Stitt, Sharon Brewer Sweatt, Cousins Rev. Robert and Marlene Tolson,** and the entire **Powell family.**

FOREWORD

Before I comment on this book, let me first say a few words about my dear Friend/Sister, Tanya Meade.

This young Woman of God is such a **tremendous** blessing to many people she comes in contact with. I must say this: She's on *FIRE* for the Lord, and she's sharing her testimony with whomever will listen.

Tanya and I met over 30 years ago through my best friend, Cathy, while we were partying at a gay bar (Tracks) in our hometown of Washington, D.C. We became close friends, but for some reason, as time went on, we lost contact with each other.

I searched the metropolitan area for her, but couldn't find any trace of her. I truly believe in my heart that our Lord and Savior, Jesus Christ, did the separation because **He** had a great work for both of us to do for Him later in life. After living my unhappy life as a lesbian, I gave my heart and life to Jesus Christ - *and He delivered me instantly!*

One day, I was on Facebook and noticed Tanya on one of our mutual friend's page. I became so excited, so I sent her a Friend's Request. Lo and behold: She accepted! *Hallelujah! Hallelujah! Hallelujah!*

We talked for a very long time. I shared with her how God saved me, that I no longer lived the gay life, and that God had set me free.

I also told her that I was in ministry and am an ordained Pastor. Tanya mentioned to me that she was also in church...but I wasn't feeling it. She had joined a *gay* church and was an ordained Deacon.

I knew what the Bible says about homosexuality in Romans 1:26-27:

"For this cause, God gave them up until vile affections: for even their women did change the natural use into that which is against nature: and likewise also the men, leaving the natural use of the woman, burned in their lust one toward another; men with men working that which is unseemly, and receiving in themselves that recompense of their error which was meet."

I also talked with our dear friend, Cathy, asking her to touch and agree with me for Tanya's deliverance.

God answered our prayers. **NOW** I understand why God didn't allow us to be in contact with each other when I searched for her. Tanya got her deliverance in August 2016. ***Hallelujah!!!***

God told me to tell Tanya that she must write a book concerning her life and that He's going to bring back to her remembrance things of the past, including her childhood.

God also said many homosexual men and lesbians will be set free and delivered from the gay lifestyle upon reading this book. ***Glory to God!***

~ Pastor Vernell Gabriel ~

From Pieces to Peace

PREFACE

From Pieces to Peace came about on the eve of my deliverance. God had already begun to give my Spiritual Godmother a download of information.

On August 24, 2016, I remember making a call. It was a Thursday evening around 6:00 p.m. Up until that time, God hadn't allowed me to say much of anything to my Spiritual Godmother.

When I made the call, I listened and spoke with anticipation of the awesome news I was about to tell her. I started out slowly and with assurance. I knew what just happened in my life was no one other than my Father in Heaven *(I tried a couple of times before, but it just didn't happen)*. I told my Spiritual Godmother I was delivered and set free from homosexuality.

God told me it was time to leave the church I was attending by revealing to me a passage of scripture. I remembered reading it before…years ago…three decades ago. I knew homosexuality was a sin. The Holy Bible calls it "an abomination before Christ".

The Lord began to show Pastor Vernell Gabriel all He planned to do with me. I couldn't say a thing. I received the prophesy. **"WOW!"** was all I could say at the time. God was definitely blowing my mind! One thing she mentioned was that she envisioned women standing in line to get this book. I'm glad God showed it to her because I would've thought He showed me someone else!

Tanya S. Meade

INTRODUCTION

The purpose of my testimony is not for me, as I have been sitting under legalistic ministries for many years. I spent many years inside the church of Pergamum. That church spends much of the time teaching about immorality of which God can't stand the sin.

The way most churches teach about being gay needs to be changed. The leaders need to come in love and not bashing. There is a way to draw people to Christ, but you need to use the Fruits of the Spirit.

A church divided cannot stand, and a church that is teaching being Lesbian, Gay, or Transgender **will** grant God's inheritance into His kingdom is *already* separated from God. Yes, they teach of God's love—as it is for everyone. Yes, it is true: God is truly love, but He is also a God of **order** and **judgment** against His churches. God loves everyone, but He hates the sin. So many people are walking in sexual immorality because they don't understand the difference.

For those of us who operate in the power of the Holy Spirit, we understand God has several names, each with a specific meaning such as:

Elohim—God of Total Power;

El Elyon—The Sovereign God;

Jehovah Jireh—The Provider; and

From Pieces to Peace

Jehovah Rapha — God the Healer...just to name a few.

If you confess with your mouth, God is quick to forgive and not remember your sin.

We can call on **Jehovah Nissi** — The Lord is my Banner. I walk in victory to be **free** from bondage, **free** from strongholds, **free** from the spirit of homosexuality, and **free** from the spirits of perversion and lust.

Understand this: God will clean you up *totally*! You will not have to worry about residue all over you because God will give you a new look and new feel to life.

The Holy Spirit arrested me while I was sitting in attendance at the second LBGTQ church. I barely had time to turn around before God pulled me out of there - with no hesitation on my part.

When God knocked on my door many years ago, I heard the call, but I didn't want to answer.

I pray this book blesses many who are walking in and living the life of a Lesbian, Gay, or Transgender. If you think you are born a certain way, take note of what Jesus says in John 3:3:

"Verily, Verily, I say unto you; You must be born again to inherit the kingdom of God."

He will give you a chance to repent and turn from the sin.

Tanya S. Meade

For three nights in a row, the Lord woke me up and led me to read and meditate on Romans 1:26-28:

"For this cause God gave them up unto vile affections, for even their women did change the natural use into that which is against nature. And likewise also the men leaving the natural use of the women burned in their lust one toward another; men with men working which is unseemly and receiving in themselves the recompense of their error which was meet - and even they did not like to retain God in their knowledge, God gave them over to reprobate mind, to do those thing which are not convenient."

God delivered me from the shame, shackles, and spirit of homosexuality and perversion. He did not intend for any of us to go to Hell.

God gave me a second chance to follow Him. He will do the same for you.

From Pieces to Peace

TABLE OF CONTENTS

DEDICATION	VI
ACKNOWLEDGEMENTS	VII
FOREWORD	IX
PREFACE	XI
INTRODUCTION	XII
THE CONCEPTION	1
THE VILLAGERS	5
TANYA FINDING HERSELF DIFFERENT	9
GROWING PAINS	15
ME, MYSELF, AND I	21
SCATTERED PIECES OF THE PUZZLE	27
THE TIGHTENED CHAIN AND MORE SCATTERED PIECES	53
CONCLUSION	91
ABOUT THE AUTHOR	97

Tanya S. Meade

CHAPTER ONE
The Conception

April 5, 1964. The day that would change Jean's life forever with the arrival of a little girl she named Tanya.

How could I possibly raise her without the help of her father? He impregnated me and left me with the responsibility of raising these two children alone. My mother said she wasn't going to raise another child after Steven — my son who is Tanya's senior by 11 years... How did I allow this conception to take place without first thinking it through? I knew he had no intention on marrying me.

Now God, I have this child. Can You help me raise Tanya without the aid of my immediate household and her father?

God answered Jean's prayer.

It was a day unlike any other. A woman I have been friends with at the hairdresser volunteered to take and raise my child. She said, "Jean, don't give your child away. I will take and raise her, and you can help out financially when you can." I will now have a home and not have to worry about would Tanya go to the right home had I put her up for adoption. She would have the presence of a man in her life - a father figure, and I would pick her up on the weekends and holidays.

I believe God answered my prayer.

Still... How would Tanya survive life in a new environment without her birth mother having a constant hand in her life? The household she was going to be raised in consisted of her Godparents and their children, Joe, Josie, Caryl, Tim, Brandon, and Martha. There is a significant distance in age between them and Tanya; between 13 and 20 years difference!

****

I felt apprehensive about being picked up by my mother and grandmother. There was a trigger that made me pull back whenever my mother came to pick me up for the weekend. Alcohol seemed to play a big role in that household. Something actually happened while spending time at my birth mother's house. I cannot clearly recall the *"what"*, but I remember being around five years old when a male 'family friend' violated me.

It's hard at five years of age to be frozen in time or suspended in fear. I began to wet the bed, and there was no explanation to explain why. Whenever my mother made an appearance, she was intoxicated. The fear would show up on my face.

As I got older, that feeling of fear was pushed back into my subconscious so I wouldn't have to remember what happened. It was so inappropriate at such a young age. *Why didn't my mother protect me from the big, bad wolf?*

The years go by, and I was in the 4th grade. Something was lurking in my brain that prompted a star-gazed look at my teacher, Ms. Wright.

The Conception

What are these thoughts swirling in my head? Where did they come from? Who put them there? Why do I feel ashamed when those thoughts enter my mind?

The ugly truth is this: I was still replaying the forbidden touch that was fused into me.

I didn't think a memory from early childhood would rush back and quicken my spirit like it was yesterday. The demons chased me in my thoughts. The bed would be soaking wet. The demons would try so hard to possess my mind, to the point I started wetting the bed.

I had my childhood ripped away by a terrible nightmare of an inappropriate touch. An ugly, distasteful hand touched my innocence.

****

There were countless others who came into my life whom aided in the stripping away of my innocence. Each played a critical role in developing the woman I had become.

"He that dwelleth in the secret place of the most High shall abide under the shadow of the Almighty.

I will say of the Lord, He is my refuge and my fortress: my God; in him will I trust."
Psalm 91:1-2 (KJV)

CHAPTER TWO
The Villagers

The beautiful, bold town of *'The Village'*. There was truly a wide variety of characters in that place! Some people have lived there for a lifetime, while others recently moved into the neighborhood.

My next-door neighbor introduced herself as 'Reese'. There was also Lynette, whom we called 'LP'. The brother and sister duo was Carl and Carla. I likened them to cats that were let loose in a large sand box. They ripped through everything they touched. If Carl touched something, it ended up broken. Carla's look was tough - like that of a tomboy - with just a **few** feminine qualities that shone through periodically.

Reese had a spunky, smart personality. She and I had fun interactions on a regular basis. A true friendship developed between Reese, LP, and me. On most days, we hung out and were the best of friends. Then, of course, there were those days when we didn't agree with each other. I can recall times when there were violent interactions. I could never figure out what those instances stemmed from. Reese always wanted to be right, no matter what. Me? I wasn't one for physical altercations.

'The Village' was one of those neighborhoods of old where everyone disciplined each other's children. As children, we couldn't do anything wrong that didn't get back to our parents.

Tanya S. Meade

I lived in a household where everyone was significantly older than me. It opened the door to always being controlled in one way or another. The closest in age to me was my sister, Martha. She was 16 years my senior. I noticed early on that the activity that surrounded her was "different".

For example, she never had boyfriends coming around. Instead, there was this one woman who hung around a lot. That same woman invited me to spend time with her in the country every summer.

I once heard that woman's grandmother refer to Martha as a *lesbian*. That term had never been mentioned before. It was almost as if it was taboo. Honey, I dared not ask grandma what the meaning of **that** word was!

Carla and Martha had some attributes that were a lot alike. What was the correlation? The appearance and tough talk. This was a little bit confusing to me. She always looked up to the older sister. Wherever she went, she would always drag me along with her.

Shane was another neighbor from up the street. I'm confused for sure now. After spending time with the girls who acted like boys, along comes Shane - the boy - with feminine qualities and a walk that would put models to shame.

The Villagers

My circle of friends became Reese, LP, and Shane. I recall the first time Shane came to my house. The look on my Godmother's face was priceless! She obviously had her own thoughts about the young man at the door with the girly attributes. After Shane left that first day, I was waiting for a speech that never came. I did feel like Shane was a good friend.

School was a different place. The people there were different as well. I heard a few boys at school call Shane a 'faggot'. Hearing that word just pushes it over the edge for me. It was like hearing the word 'lesbian' coming out of my grandmother's mouth about my godsister. I soon found myself pulling away from Shane at school. I began taking notice of the differences in people.

"Surely he shall deliver thee from the snare of the fowler, and from the noisome pestilence.

He shall cover thee with his feathers, and under his wings shalt thou trust: his truth shall be thy shield and buckler."
Psalm 91:3-4 (KJV)

CHAPTER THREE
Tanya Finding Herself Different

How is it that I could find myself feeling different than everyone else? I felt like I was in a bubble, and the rest of the world was walking past while taking a little peep inside.

The feeling was overwhelming at times. At my young age, how could I feel so inadequate and out of place? All of my friends were interested in boys, and their hormones were raging. I liked boys, but my reaction when around them was so different.

The conversations with the boys were unlike what my peers experienced and talked about. I felt the oddness in the 'boy conversation', but would make myself act like the other girls acted and talk about things the other girls talked about when in the presence of boys — with sex being the primary topic. The pressure to conform at that age was immense! At 10 years old, it felt like the right thing to do.

I can recall one of the boys I liked, but I also remember liking the girl he was playing around with.

The lightbulb moment hit me like a ton of bricks: I discovered in that moment that **MY** hormones were responding to the female gender.

I had quite the conundrum. How can the feelings I was having dissipate or diminish? After all, my parents raised me to be a Christian! My transition was sure to be alarming to my peers, both in and out of school.

I had to find a way to keep this information locked away in my mind. My birth mother and godparents would surely disown me if that information ever got out.

Church was the usual: same service, same people. A new young lady had joined our church and the choir. There was an awareness of her that I felt immediately. My "gay-dar" went off. "Gay-dar" is that thing inside that goes off when you recognize someone who gives an unspoken sense that he or she is just like you.

Oh my God! *I had to deal with this feeling - not only in school and the neighborhood, but now in **church**?* The walls were closing in. My breath came in short spurts. I was pleading to God: **PLEASE** don't let me get exposed!

The new girl wore dresses, but her walk? Her walk had a shifty, pimp-style to it. Cool papa up the street with a cane and a three-piece suit type of style.

My brain felt like it was being divided into two people. Poor me. I had to juggle this alternate personality just to hide my truth.

As the years advanced, I kept my secret quiet and hidden deep inside. I dated boys as a way of keeping my feelings towards girls on the down-low.

Tanya Finding Herself Different

When it came time to attend high school, there was one young man I thought I could really like and be quite content with. He was a state wrestling champion. I thought, "*What a perfect cover! No one would ever know my secret, and he qualified with those things I was seeking in a boyfriend!*"

It wouldn't dare be that simple, would it?

I began to notice I had some emerging feelings for my Math teacher, "Mrs. G". Believe it or not, I found it awkward to have a boyfriend who would walk me to class and try to kiss me. I felt like I was cheating on Mrs. G!

Soon, the emotional separation began to happen between my boyfriend and I. I couldn't handle the strain of keeping the façade of a relationship going, knowing in my heart it was a lie.

One day, Mrs. G announced she was leaving the area. In that moment, I felt like someone ripped the skin right off of my body without any sedatives. There was a classmate by the name of 'Weedie' who teased me by yelling out, "*Hey, Tanya! Are you going to kiss Mrs. G goodbye when she leaves?*"

I felt the floor drop from underneath me.

Did the rest of the class hear her? Or was it all just my imagination?

Mrs. G asked if anyone was interested in raising her finch bird. I raised my hand and then stated I needed to discuss it with my godmother - who agreed to let me raise the bird.

On the day we picked up the bird, I was very nervous about going to her house. As she exited the house with the bird in the cage, I had to do a heart-check. I wondered: Would I get the kiss Weedie mentioned? Or will just a hug suffice?

MEMORY MOMENT: I had such a huge crush on Mrs. G, I ended up taking her class twice.

What was happening in my mind? Life has thrown many horrible spins, one right after the other. It feels like another person - a virtual stranger - is trying to emerge from my inner-being. It was not a good feeling, either.

Debra and Addie (my two closest friends in junior high) noticed something wasn't quite right with me. One of them was flaunting over a jock named Michael. He seemed to be having an identity crisis while trying to decide what color skin he would best identify with. Being honest, I just wasn't interested in him…or genuinely interested in *ANY* boy, for that matter.

Tanya Finding Herself Different

For me, I surmised that if I got more involved in church activities, the thoughts of same-sex attraction would go away. Well, I was wrong. Going to church was simply a band-aid for a greater problem. Two other girls who sang on the choir were struggling with their identity - just as I was - but they were not struggling with who they were. Why did I have such a hard time?

Deep down inside, I felt it wasn't the right path for me. Only time would tell...

Why these growing pains?

"Thou shalt not be afraid for the terror by night; nor for the arrow that flieth by day;

Nor for the pestilence that walketh in darkness; nor for the destruction that wasteth at noonday.

A thousand shall fall at thy side, and ten thousand at thy right hand; but it shall not come nigh thee.

Only with thine eyes shalt thou behold and see the reward of the wicked."
Psalm 91:5-8 (KJV)

CHAPTER FOUR
Growing Pains

On most weekends, I spent time at my mother's and grandmother's house. My mother would always fix breakfast for me and have the Bible opened to *Psalm 23* while she did so. That was the first passage of scripture I actually memorized on my own. My relationship with my grandmother was strained, and I really couldn't understand why. I suppose it could be related to the fact that my mother didn't follow her instruction for giving me away. My mother decided she didn't want to get rid of me - perhaps because God dealt with her in that regard.

The household where I lived and my mother's house felt pulled apart. Communication wasn't working. There were times I felt like I wish I wasn't born.

I just wanted us to be one, big family. The personalities on both sides were very strong, but not as much for my mother. She was a quiet, praying woman. It seemed like she was always in deep thought. I dared not ask, "*Mom, what is wrong?*" I must admit: I was scared of what her response would be.

Being torn between two households was indeed a challenging time for me. It didn't help that my mind was trying to come to grips with clearly identifying the feelings I was experiencing while, at the same time, understanding who my body was craving.

Dealing with my grandmother was very difficult and trying. She was very cut throat and to-the-point. Balancing that relationship was very painful at times. There were also times the relationship was strained between her and my mother. Grandmother ruled and reigned her house, without question.

I vowed I would never let myself be exposed. Who I was growing into and the feelings I was having about other girls must never be exposed. After hearing my grandmother call Martha a *lesbian*, there was no way I was even considering spilling the beans in **that** household!

The only thing I could do was try to gain a sense of normalcy in my life. Boyfriends had to become a focal point, and I enlisted the help of my friend Shane to find a boyfriend. Well, Shane introduced me to Allen. All went well for a little while - that was until I noticed Shane and Allen were hanging out way too much.

Soon enough, Allen's mannerisms began to mimic Shane's. I started asking questions and, after finally introducing him to friends and family as my boyfriend, the truth about him came to the surface: Shane revealed Allen was gay.

My mouth dropped open. **Why the lie?**

Growing Pains

I didn't stay mad very long. In fact, a friendship developed between Allen and me. Besides, the car he drove — a Bradley GT with suicide doors *(doors that raise up instead of out)* — was really nice-looking. Maybe that was the **real** reason I dated him...because he had an interesting car. Allen caused first heartbreak while I was in the 11th grade. Finding out he was gay truly broke my heart!

My next boyfriend was a grade behind me. His name was Duke. He had attributes like Prince the singer. In fact, a poster I had in my room of Prince, my godfather Joe made me take down. He thought the image was Duke.

This was such a confusing time in my life. I shied away from getting serious with anyone, but I wanted to have fun at the same time. Between spending time with Duke, there was another boyfriend from my bowling days who had an interest in me.

Still...

That girl 'thing' was in the back of my mind, even though I thought it was just a phase.

The last couple years of school, we were required to take a vocational course. Girls were taking classes like Medical Assistant and Cosmetology. I really couldn't concentrate on the course I chose: Nursing. I knew those secret thoughts of mine had to remain just that: secret.

In the midst of it all, Duke accused me of dating him only because I needed a prom date.

Duke was the only boy out of many sisters. I knew early on our relationship wasn't going to last, especially because I had a crush on one of his sisters *(uh-oh)*.

I looked forward to visiting his house primarily because I wanted to see one of his sisters. It was an awful feeling, pretending to like someone while lusting after another.

One day, Duke tossed out the courtesy of asking what we would be doing that week. He liked to quickly assume that all of my attention would be centered on him. Well, I decided to attend a swimming party instead of going out with him.

You can only imagine what happened... As a consequence of my "disobedience", our relationship came to an abrupt end.

I wondered why every guy I got involved with tried one of two things: to either dominate me and my time or pierce my virginity. *Yes: I was still a virgin.*

At one point, I even tried dating someone 10 years my senior, thinking it would be different than dealing with younger guys. I met this man during my days of bowling in the league. He was very much established and independent. **"JACKPOT!"** I thought to myself.

My father wasn't feeling the older man at all. The man wanted to take me to Atlantic City for an entire weekend once. My father said, *"NO! A day trip will suffice."*

Growing Pains

I quickly learned **that** man wanted the same thing the younger guys wanted: to lay claim to my virginity. He was even bold enough to tell me he didn't even want to use protection! The sirens in my head began to sound the alarm. "*Oh! He's the town idiot*", I thought. "*Who do I look like? Ubu the Fool? Sex without protection spelled out 'baby out of wedlock'!*"

"*Why is this happening? Young guys are losers, and older men are no better*", I thought. It began to settle in my spirit that he wasn't going to spend money on me unless he had something to show for it. He would come around in his Corvette or on his cruiser. It was exciting…at first.

The growing pains were simply way too much at this stage in my young adult life.

I began to get bored with this older guy. Emotionally, everything was adding up to the same thing: Whether young or old, the male persuasion was immature.

I thought, ***"It's time to do me!"***

"Because thou hast made the Lord, which is my refuge, even the most High, thy habitation;

There shall no evil befall thee, neither shall any plague come nigh thy dwelling.

For he shall give his angels charge over thee, to keep thee in all thy ways.

They shall bear thee up in their hands, lest thou dash thy foot against a stone."
Psalm 91:9-12 (KJV)

CHAPTER FIVE
Me, Myself, and I

Once I graduated high school, the next adventure was college. The summer before was a time to determine both what I really wanted in my personal life and future career. Since taking vocational classes in high school, it looked like nursing was on the horizon.

I decided I wanted to start hanging out with Sally. Sally and I were friends who exchanged VHS tapes on the weekend of the things we would record during the week. One day, Sally said, "*Hey! We need to start living our lives and having some fun!*"

We decided to check out the club scene on Fridays and weekends. It became our regular routine. We would find a club and gel the atmosphere. There was one club in particular we would frequent often. It was called "Michelle's". On Friday evening, I would get "the call" from Sally that went something like this:

"*Hey, girl! You ready to hang out and see some new faces?*"

This went on for about a year, even during college. We met some new people, became friendly, and decided to hang out together. We all knew the place to be in Temple Hills, Maryland. Across the street from the famous club was a strip club for women to watch men.

Every place that Sally and I ventured into, people would try to figure out our card. The men couldn't figure out why they couldn't get with us. She and I had no strings attached. I wasn't looking for a hookup, and neither was Sally. We had a good time talking trash to the guys and then leaving them wondering.

One day, Sally and I were with the rest of the crew and decided to venture outside of the club in Temple Hills. A club called 'Tracks' entered into our conversations. Sally and I had never heard of 'Tracks' before. Our friend Jaz said he wanted to ride along. Five of us ended up heading into D.C. to check out 'Tracks'. The club was located in the southeastern part of Washington D.C. It was huge and engulfed a couple of city blocks.

All of us were in awe. 'Tracks' had a room that played music videos, a wading pool with a couple of grills at poolside, and a dance floor unlike anything we had ever seen before in our area of town. Walking into that club, something inside of me ignited a spark. The song that was playing at the time was Animotion's *"Obsession"*. The song had a mesmerizing effect on me.

Jaz and I walked throughout the club. I took notice that he, too, was lit up and ready to party. We both experienced a moment, as if to say, **"We are home! This is the club we've been looking for!"**

One of the signs on the front door read, **"This club is a Gay establishment, run and owned by a Gay man."** Another stated they didn't close until 6:00 a.m.

Me, Myself, and I

Within its walls, everyone seemed to be free, as if they were on a drug that was being pumped into the club's air conditioning system.

My bestie looked at me and smiled. In that smile, it said that she was uncomfortable there. I had no idea how I would tell Sally I had no desire to go back to Club Michelle's anymore. 'Tracks' was the place for me. My mind was moving a million miles a minute, trying to absorb the entire scene before me.

I asked the woman who was collecting the entry fee how long the club had been open. She stated a little less than a year. She went on to explain that one needed a membership to join the club.

"*Oh my*", I thought. "*This club must be very exclusive because you need a **membership** to get in!*" I inquired about the cost of membership. I learned the 'Enthusiastic Card' was $100.00 for one year. I asked, "*What do you get for $100?*" The response was pleasing: Free crabs on your birthday, access to the cookouts that were given on the outside patio, and free drinks during certain events.

There were no less than seven bars inside of 'Tracks' with attentive bartenders and barbacks. The outside of the club had a wooden fence, a volleyball net and sand that laid the foundation for a fun game, and the wading pool was off to the side.

'Tracks' was unlike any other club I had **EVER** seen, and I had been to quite a few bars up to that point. Club 'Tracks' exposed me to a new trend of partying. You didn't have to be dressed up to enter into the atmosphere. Whatever you were wearing was just fine. *"Wow!"* I thought. *"I don't have to put on heels and nice pair of slacks to come here!"*

I saw people with shorts, flip-flops, spandex, t-shirts, jeans...you name it, people were wearing it. There was also a mixture of different races. It was an awesome setting. The place was open seven days a week, too.

*"When do they **rest**?"* I thought. *"I will definitely be back!"*

Once the weekend was over and the start of a new week was ushered in, I couldn't wait to hear from Sally to get her thoughts about the weekend and our new club discovery. Her take was on the club was a bit vague, as she stated it really wasn't her cup of tea. She stated she could tell, though, that it caught my attention as well as Jaz's.

I couldn't stop thinking about that club. I wondered when I was going to be able to visit again and who was going to go with me. Since Jaz seemed like he had a great time, I had myself a new dance partner! 'Tracks' would definitely be on my radar for future events and play dates!

'Tracks' seemed to be a place that plagued me. *Why did I constantly think about that place?* It was as if it had an invisible magnet, drawing people in. *Could it be the Pandora's Box that might provide the answers I have been seeking to those nagging questions about my sexuality?*

Me, Myself, and I

I knew asking Sally to go back was definitely out of the question. She was a person who had no desire to hang out with people who were not "like her". She often used the phrase, **"I wish a b***h would!"** Right off the bat, I knew not to push that cart. I would ultimately find a new hanging partner. My feelings were not going away.

There was a knock at my door. Well, well, well…guess who decided to visit? Shane! The thought went off like a lightbulb. *"I have found my tour guide to the new hangout spot!"* Me, Myself, and I are revving it up! Shane was the **perfect** person to help me understand what was happening in my mind. Surely, he had been to 'Tracks' on many occasions and knows the ins and outs of how things are run. It was the perfect opportunity to discuss the club with him.

He brought me up to speed quickly. Everybody and their brother must be hanging out at the new club. It was nothing like The Classics, Chapter 3, Hangars Club, or Michelle's where everyone spent their time trying to fit in. 'Tracks' was truly a judgment-free zone!

Hanging out with Sally, I didn't see much of my other friends from school. Reese, Lynette, and everyone else seemed to be doing their own thing. I would see Reese hanging out with Everett and Dawn every once in a while. I visited a few times, but when I did, Reese was standoffish and hardly ever in the mood to answer questions. I once saw some birth control pills on her dresser. I assumed they were there for a reason.

Sometimes, Shane would be over there talking to Dawn and Reese. *Hmm...I wonder what that was about?* I didn't give it much thought, though. It was none of my business. Whatever the 'secret society' had going on didn't involve me.

I had enough going on in my own brain, trying to make sense of the scattered pieces. The more I tried to figure it all out, the more interesting things took a direction out of the way.

After hanging out with Sally at the clubs and being introduced to 'Tracks', what's next?

CHAPTER SIX
Scattered Pieces of the Puzzle

I was eager to check out the club, but scared at the same time. Reality began to set in.

What happens next?

The first time I went to 'Tracks', I was with my straight friends on a night when not many people were at the club. I had to wonder: *What would it be like on a night if I decided to attend with my gay friend, Shane?*

I was about to call Shane when he showed up at my house. He started the conversation with, *"What's been going on?"* I mentioned I had been hanging out with Sally and ventured out to D.C. one night to go clubbing - a change from the same, boring clubs in Temple Hills.

Shane always got this look in his eyes with an inquisitive or surprised facial expression.

"Boy, you make me sick", I said. He laughed.

"Don't keep me hanging! Spill the beans, girl!"

I rolled my eyes and began to tell the story about the club Sally and I went to a few nights ago. When I mentioned the club's name was 'Tracks', his eyes practically popped out of their sockets. With his hands on his hips, he urged me on with, **"DO TELL!"** He knew right away that I liked the club by the excitement I displayed while describing it to him.

Shane looked at me glassy-eyed and asked, "*Chile, what are you saying to me?*" I stood there for a second, scared to move my lips. After a moment of awkwardness passed, I asked, "*Have you been to the club I just mentioned?*" With a crazy laugh to accompany his response, he stated, **"Of course! If it's gay, I've been!"**

Then, things suddenly got real juicy.

He said, "*Well, did you know Reese goes there? I've also seen Dawn there, too.*"

"Oh, really?" I asked. Excitement flooded my eyes. "*Is she gay?*"

He looked slightly amused. "*The two of them are thick as thieves. If I had to guess, I would say 'yes'.*"

His next question came out before I had a chance to ask it myself. "*Would you like to go with me sometime? I will take you on a night that you would feel more comfortable.*"

I knew I couldn't turn that offer down.

Why was I feeling all schoolgirlish all of a sudden? Was it because I knew someone really close to me who might be 'playing on a different team'?

"*What night are you thinking about going?*"

"*Wednesday. It's considered 'straight night'.*"

I agreed to go that coming Wednesday night.

Scattered Pieces of the Puzzle

The big day came with the utmost swiftness. Wow! Wednesday already? I flipped through my closet, trying to find the perfect outfit for the occasion. *Hmm... Should I ask my mom to use her car for the evening?* I suppose I should inquire with Shane to see if he would be driving. He stated he would and will pick me up around 8:00 p.m.

When we arrived at 'Tracks', the feel was a little different than the first time I was there. I felt a freeness in the atmosphere, but I was still scared at the same time. Unlike before, a lot more people were there. Someone in line was talking about getting their Enthusiastic Card because the club was running a special that night: Get the $100 Enthusiastic Card for only $25.00. We stood in line for what seemed like forever. While waiting, I observed the crowd around me. There were some interesting characters there...to say the least.

There was one particular woman who was working that night as a barback. She seemed a little too aggressive for my taste. I was clinging to Shane like my life depended on it.

Shane was laughing at me. I didn't think anything was funny. I thought to myself, "*Do all of the women here act the same way? Do they all look like her? She seemed to be overly-friendly.*" Shane must've sensed my unease, as he suddenly responded to my unspoken thoughts. "*She smells fresh fish.*"

I was confused. "*What? Fish??*"

He laughed uncontrollably at my innocent ignorance. "*It means she knows who is a regular versus a newbie.*"

As we stood in line, I continued to observe my surroundings. There were so many interesting people, and one could easily tell: They were **FREE**! I had never seen so many men with more female qualities than women in my life! 'Tracks' was definitely not the usual club. I really appreciated being able to wear whatever I wanted with no one around to judge my outward appearance. I was getting comfortable.

Once we purchased our cards, we took a tour of the club - both inside and outside. I was introduced to so many people, including Ann, the Club Manager. I was just taking it all in. The music was off the chain, with a blend of mixed tracks and dee-jaying techniques. The video room was located in the smaller side of the club. There was also an area where we could hang up our coats.

I saw some interesting things for sale in the case and asked Shane about these party favor-looking things. He suggested I wouldn't have an interest in them. They were called "poppers". They were recreational drugs that give the user a few seconds of an exotic high. He was right: Not my cup of tea - especially something I had never even heard of before tonight.

In the back of my mind, I wondered if Reese and Dawn were going to show up while we were there. As the night wore on, there was no sign of my friends.

Scattered Pieces of the Puzzle

Shane and I took to the dance floor, showing off our dance moves. It felt so free to dance while knowing no one cared or stared at me. I turned around towards Shane, then all of a sudden, I felt someone rubbing their body all on my butt. I turned back around and…

OH MY GOD! It was the **WOMAN** who kept trying to flirt with me while we were standing in line!

I freaked out and ran off the dance floor. Shane followed me, laughing hysterically. *"What's wrong?"* he asked. *"Look: I ain't ready for those shenanigans!"* was my reply.

That aggressiveness was too fast for comfort. I wanted to check out the scene, but not like **THAT**! People just roll up on you like that? **Wow!**

The lady found us and apologized. Shane explained to her that I was straight. "*Oh. Sorry, again*", she said with disappointment. She went on to introduce herself. "*Hi! I'm Sherron.*"

We exchanged brief pleasantries. All the while, my heart was beating a million miles a minute. Phew! I dodged a bullet.

"I can't believe you were laughing! That wasn't funny, Shane!"

"It was funny! If you could have seen your face, Tanya!"

We continued to peruse the club, walking from one side to the other. I do believe they called what we were doing "cruising". Shane said he liked to go to different places cruising guys. I asked him where else he goes, and he stated the Pentagon.

"**WHAT?** *Are you serious?*" I asked in awe.

"*Hey, you would be surprised how many men you see around there looking for a down-low quickie!*"

As we were walking through the club, I saw one of my old boyfriends. Now I see why things didn't work out with us. I wasn't his 'type'. His boyfriend had the same name as him. One was using the proper pronunciation, the other the short version. *Hmm… To think they named a horse after him.* I had to laugh. Well, one thing's for sure: That revelation made the night even more interesting!

Shane and I stayed a little while longer, danced, and laughed a little bit more. The time came to call it a night. I was tired and was a bit overwhelmed from the experience. "*Wow! I thought men were bad, but these women are no joke! Too d**m aggressive for me. I'm sure there has to be women who are softer and easy-going*", I pondered.

I wanted to get another stab at the Reese thing. Reese wasn't budging. It played in the back of my mind about what Shane revealed about her. By now, I'm sure Reese suspected Shane had ran his big mouth about what he saw. It was time for him to get cussed out by Dawn.

Scattered Pieces of the Puzzle

Shane told me Dawn and Reese tried to read him with their finger-popping and neck-moving attitudes. I have no doubt all Shane did was read them back, roll his eyes, and sashay down the street back home.

All throughout the week that followed my visit to 'Tracks', I thought about my time there. I knew I had plans to hook up with Pernell, the guy I was seeing on and off. I was getting a little bored with him. He simply wasn't doing it for me anymore. He seemed like all he wanted was to be the first to pop my cherry - and **THAT** wasn't going to happen. I will admit, though: He tried one time, and it was painful. I was not interested in that happening again. Besides, he didn't want to use protection. He actually stated he had confidence in his pull-out method! **Ha!**

Shane told me about another night I might be interested in at 'Tracks'. The last Tuesday of every month is "Women's Night". *Hmm... I guess it couldn't be that bad.* Maybe - just maybe - it would include other women who weren't quite so aggressive.

That Tuesday night arrived, and it was time to get the party started. I was ready to check out this bomb-biggity night that Shane assured me was 'just for me'. When we pulled up to the club, wow! My eyes almost jumped out of my head!

There were mostly women standing in line. I could tell right away the night would definitely be different than any other night that I had been there. Something peculiar was in the air. It was a smell of excitement.

On this night, they had different prices to enter the club. For those who made it there before 8:00 p.m., they entered for free. We had to pay to get in because it was after that time when we arrived.

The way the women were piling into the club was indicative that it had to be the best night or at least one of them. The men who accompanied the women had to remain on the video side. Only women were allowed in the big section. I felt like a kid in a candy store. There were so many pieces of candy and flavors to choose from!

"Dang! All of these women cannot be gay! Where do they live? Are they imported from another state? Where do they hide? Some look really cute. There are all types: tall, short, fat, skinny, boy-looking, and others real hard-looking - almost mannish. Some have on heels and dresses. Others, shorts and tennis shoes. Still others, ties and slacks. So much confusion", I thought.

I didn't understand why women wanted to be like men. I thought the reason for being with a woman was because a woman didn't want to be with a man.

There were women hanging outside playing volleyball in the sand. Some were playing in tank tops or just their sports bras.

I sought out Shane on the video side and hung out with him for a bit.

Scattered Pieces of the Puzzle

I took notice that more and more women poured into the club. It looked like a few hundred women. I overheard someone say, **"There has to be at least 2,000 women in here tonight!"** It was literally a smorgasbord of women!

I soon noticed that women were looking at me. I had a sense of heightened excitement and fear all rolled into one. A random thought flashed through my mind: *What do gay women do together?*

Out of the corner of my eye, who did I see coming into the club? Reese and Dawn. Got you now, ladies! **Busted!** They see me and immediately don the deer-in-the-headlights look. We asked each other the same question at the same time:

*"What are **YOU** doing here?"*

I thought about the birth control pills I saw on Reese's dresser. Well, there goes **THAT** theory! I don't think you need birth control pills when you are clearly in a girl-on-girl relationship. Neither party is getting pregnant by the other!

Instead of causing a scene, we all grouped together, left the area, and walked around the club, taking in all that was happening. Women were there. Girls were there. Whatever you want to call them, they were there. Some looked very young, and others looked like they should be at home in the bed already. The excitement of being in that crowd caused a sense of giddiness among the party-goers. It was becoming apparent that it was going to be a long night of dancing, partying, and females getting to know one another.

I asked one of the bartenders, "*Is it like this* **EVERY** *ladies' night?*" The response I received was favorable and to my liking.

I recall a moment when this one woman entered the club and walked as if she owned it. She was about 5'6" or so and walked as if she had her own runway as she cat-walked through the club. I asked Shane, "*Who is that?*" As he often does, his reply came with laughter. "*Chile, I don't know! Just another fish!*" I remembered seeing her on the dance floor on the larger side of the club. She was obviously flip-flopping from one side to the other...a true attention-seeker and attention-getter!

Whatever that girl had going on, she gained the attention of many people. She had a flyness about herself. She exuded an appreciation for life and what it had to offer. Wow! She had that confidence thing down-packed! She obviously knew who she was and how to have fun. The cute boy-looking girls followed her around. I was sure one of them must have been 'with her'.

There were a lot of black women in attendance. Perhaps 'Tracks' was the only place they could be free to unmask who they really are. Just think: We go home and hide what we like to do because it's not accepted in our homes, schools, and jobs.

Scattered Pieces of the Puzzle

I couldn't help but think: *What would my mother think if she knew the 'real me'?* Oh my God! Just the thought of telling my mom... Hell to the **NO**! It's probably just a matter of time before she starts asking questions, knowing gay Shane is at the house almost every day or every other day. His feminine ways give him away completely. I hate to say this, but I sometimes feel embarrassed around him. Switching his little, skinny butt comes natural for him. Even his laughter is girly-pronounced.

It was getting late and time to call it a night. We had a great time in the 'fish bowl'. As we prepared to leave, we noticed the festivities were picking up, not sizzling out. Smiling and laughing with Shane on the way out, I was already thinking about my next visit. Whether gay or straight, everyone had a good time at 'Tracks'. It had an amusement park feel and was great for one's adrenalin.

There was one small downside. The location was not the greatest. It was wise of party-goers to employ the services of the street and homeless people to watch over their cars while at the club. They never charged much; just a bag of chips and a soda. Others needed money to feed their drug habits.

I couldn't believe I had to wait another **month** for the next ladies' event, but before I knew it, that month had come! It was off to the club again! I asked Shane to go with me this time. The minute we walked in, he knew a few of the people on the video side. A few ladies introduced themselves and asked if I would be interested in hanging out with them. I agreed. One of the ladies was named Cathy (Cat). It was nice meeting new people.

I ventured the club on my own for a while, checking out the new faces and seeing some from last month's event. A young woman who looked to be about my age was smiling and staring at me. I was a little nervous and excited at the same time. She approached me and introduced herself.

"*Hello. My name is Carrie, but my friends call me CJ.*" She was quite different from the women who have tried to approach me previously. I proceeded with caution.

There was an older, nice-looking woman with CJ. I couldn't tell whether they were 'just friends' or more. CJ and I walked off to a quiet place to talk and get to know each other a little better. We exchanged phone numbers and went our separate ways.

Scattered Pieces of the Puzzle

Later, the older woman with CJ was introduced to me as her friend, Anna. We shook hands. There was definitely a shyness about the whole meeting. Anna's soft eyes were checking me out from head to toe. I couldn't help but think, *"Is this CJ's mama or auntie? They can't be anything more than family or friends with the way she was obviously looking at me."* Anna egged CJ on to keep me entertained with conversation. What was up with the whispering and cannery grinning between the two of them?

The next day, my phone rang. It was CJ on the other end saying what a great time she had. She began asking me some questions. One of the questions asked was, *"Are you gay?"* The response was deafening. *"No. I'm straight."* There was a long pause before she continued. *"Can I call you back?"* I replied, *"Sure! No problem."*

What just happened to our conversation? My answer immediately shut her down. Shortly after, CJ called back. She stated accusatorily, *"Wow. You didn't tell me you were straight."*

"Well, you never asked me. Plus, that was only the second time I visited the club with my friend, Shane."

After that, the conversation took a turn for the better. She actually invited me over to her house! The nervousness really gained steam, with sweat pouring from my forehead. I had to laugh to myself. I had to call Shane to explain what just happened.

"Well, Ms. Thing: You were invited to a fish fry at Ms. CJ's house! So, what are you going to do?"

I had to remove the frog from my throat before replying. "*What do you think, Shane? I don't know. I'm really new at all of this.*"

"*If you really like what you feel, go. If you just want to get to know her, go.*"

A very large lump formed in my throat. All types of thoughts went flying through my head. I couldn't think straight - no pun intended. Sweat beads formed all over again. I never had these types of reactions with any of my boyfriends, except when they wanted sex and I wasn't interested in obliging.

I picked up the phone and made the call. "*Hello. Can I speak to Carrie?*"

"*Speaking*", the voice on the other end replied.

"*Umm* [clearing my throat], *when would you like me to come over to your house?*"

"*Friday is a good day. Can you make it then?*"

"*Sure!*"

"*Well, I will cook dinner. Do you have a taste for anything in particular?*"

"*I really don't have a preference. Oh. I don't eat liver.*"

"*I wasn't going to cook that.*" A light laughter flowed from each of us. "*Do you eat spaghetti?*"

Scattered Pieces of the Puzzle

"Yes. That's one of my favorite dishes!"

"Great! Let me give you my address." (I noticed she lived relatively close - about 10 minutes away.) *"I'll see you on Friday!"*

My anticipation went through the roof! I immediately called Shane back, thinking that maybe it was too soon to commit going to her house. By the time Shane finished talking me through my emotions, I felt better about the upcoming visit to CJ's home.

Wouldn't you know it? The week **FLEW** by! Friday came, and my heart was racing so hard, it was about to bust out of my chest!

Again, the thought came: My past relationships with men didn't cause my heart to race like that…**EVER**.

Now, my mind was racing as well! I had to find a cute outfit to suit the occasion. You know…that first impressions thing. Well, come to think of it, I already made my lasting first impression. I wondered if I was conquest of CJ's to see if she could get herself a straight girl.

I had to purposefully stop my mind from wondering and just **GO**. Go, have a good time, and see what happens. I jumped into my car and headed over to CJ's house. That was a very short 10-minute trip!

When I arrived, she met me at the door wearing a t-shirt and shorts. She was a hippie and had a nice butt. Wait. *What? I was checking out her body parts?* **YIKES!**

She introduced me to her mother and two brothers, then took me to her room and shut the door behind us. Right away, I was nervous with her mom and brothers close by. I knew our time together on that night was just to get to know each other better and for me to begin feeling comfortable around her, but still…her family was uncomfortably close.

CJ stated dinner was almost ready. Good, because I was hungry! I had to laugh to myself on that one. Just as we discussed previously, spaghetti was the meal of choice. It was an easy and fast meal to prepare. Had the situation been reversed and she was at my home, I would have fixed the same meal.

The evening went well - so well, we actually made plans to see each other again. Her family seemed to be nice and receptive of my presence. It was also good to know she and her brother were fans of the Dallas Cowboys NFL team. That was something awesome that we had in common.

I couldn't wait to tell Shane about my first date with CJ. I stopped by his house the following day, and we giggled about my story and talked a lot of trash. He was very inquisitive. He, of course, wanted to know what I thought of her. I explained that she seemed nice and that I wanted to take things really slow. After all, it was all new to me. The next thing he said I "heard" but didn't really "hear", as it was the farthest thing from my mind:

Scattered Pieces of the Puzzle

He inquired about whether or not I could see CJ and I having sex.

That whole sex thing? I wasn't even familiar with my own body. I didn't know what I wanted or would enjoy.

I had to dismiss the thought for the moment and cross that bridge when the time came.

CJ and I continued to see each other regularly. We would meet up at the club or ride together, depending on the event and whose car was available. I was introduced to many other people in her circle of friends.

My parents were heading out of town, which meant I would have the house to myself — or so I thought.

Before I decided to tinker with the homosexual lifestyle, there was one gentleman I used to mess with. He and I dated a few times, and things between us were not gelling. One day, while CJ was at my house, I saw his motorcycle coming up the road. At first, I didn't think anything of it. As he got closer, I began to feel nervous — hoping he didn't know about my lifestyle change.

CJ and I were standing outside when he stopped to speak. "*I haven't heard from you in a while*", he said. I didn't know how to respond to that. "*I've been busy*", I said. He looked at me, then at CJ, then back to me to gain some clarity about why he had not seen me.

CJ gave him this look that clearly stated she did not like men. It was really an awkward moment. He soon tired of trying to pull out information and getting nowhere. I believe he came to the conclusion it wasn't going to happen with he and I again, so he jumped on his bike and drove away.

His absence left me to contend with the following conversation from CJ:

"I guess by now, I would have to consider us an item since we have been hanging and dating for a little while now."

She asked a few questions and learned I had never been with a man sexually, let alone a woman. Yep! I was still a virgin! I briefly explained that the man who just left wanted to be the first, and I wouldn't allow it to happen. I wasn't entertaining the thought of children, as I was barely an adult myself at the time.

Once we went back into the house, we went downstairs to the den to continue talking. Before I knew it, she felt comfortable enough to make a move on me. She kissed me to gauge what my response would be. **WHOA!** Well, I kissed her back - and it seemed like Mother Nature took its course. We ended up making out…and one thing led to another.

Scattered Pieces of the Puzzle

CJ didn't want to go too far and fast with me. We ended up partially naked. Suddenly, I heard a knock at the door. Oh my God! It was my aunt and cousin! I freaked out and didn't know how to respond. My aunt rang the doorbell. CJ and I dressed and straightened up the room hurriedly. I was trying to think of what to say about the delay in answering the door. The first thing that came to mind was that we were watching TV and fell asleep on the sofa.

My cousin looked at me and then CJ. It was like she already knew that was a lie and we were caught. I introduced CJ to them, and she quickly rushed out of the door after the introductions. My aunt and cousin stayed around for a while and we chit-chatted.

Later on, I spoke to CJ and we laughed about the situation. It was truly a scary moment for me. She asked me if my mother knew about my sexuality. I said, "*Are you kidding? No freaking way! She would have a heart attack and die!*" Meanwhile, our relationship continued to deepen.

The end of summer was approaching and school was about to start again. I was attending the University of the District of Columbia. I remember meeting a young lady at school, but I can't recall how the connection between she and I happened. I do know she was looking to establish new friendships.

Her name was Leslie. Something about her said to me, *"She is just like you"*. After talking to her and getting to know each other at school, I felt comfortable enough to introduce her to CJ and Anna. We all made plans to meet up at Mr. Henry's - a nice hangout spot for the gay community to eat and drink.

I purposely introduced Leslie to Anna, thinking they would hit it off. They exchanged information and went out together a few times, but Anna said there was no chemistry. That relationship went nowhere.

CJ and Leslie's friendship had a different feel to it. When I would call CJ for us to make plans, there was something in her tone that said, *"I have company"*. It grew to the point where I felt as if I needed to call her secretary to make appointments to get together. When I spoke on our sex life, she would always say, *"You want to do that **NOW**?"*

Thoughts ran through my head. *"What's wrong with this picture? This kept happening too much to me."*

One day while I was at CJ's, I noticed a journal she kept. I asked her about its contents. She said it was personal and that I wasn't allowed to read it. *"Okay. No problem. I bet everything I want to know about what's going on is in there"*, I thought.

Scattered Pieces of the Puzzle

I was no longer feeling the love from CJ. She was obviously getting bad advice from Anna. CJ looked up to Anna, a woman who was much older than both of us. Anna could pull all types of women - if she wanted to. She was a tiny, aggressive feminine woman who was the mother of a daughter whom she was extremely tough on. I felt sorry for the girl. When I would call CJ, she was always on the phone with Anna. Our time together lessened and lessened. My heart felt like it was breaking.

I introduced CJ to another one of my friends who had come back on the scene from past bowling tournaments. Her name was Renee. Renee, Leslie, CJ, and I would hang out occasionally. CJ and Renee seemed to be getting close. Was my imagination playing tricks on me? Was I turning into the jealous girlfriend from hell? I didn't like the feeling. My stomach was in knots all the time. I hated to make the call, fearing rejection.

Now, I didn't have any solid proof that anything was happening. I just hated having the uncertainty of it all floating in my spirit. CJ and I started getting into arguments about her not spending time with me. When she said the following, it sent chills up my spine:

"I need some space."

That was a horrible time in my life. I found myself doing things that were outside of my norm. For example, I would drive over to her house and park in the lot, just to see if I could catch her doing something. I didn't really know what I was expecting to catch her doing. I could have gone up to and just knocked on the door, but I didn't do that because I didn't really want to know who or what is on the other side with her.

Renee and I would get together from time to time and go out to the club or some other outing. I took notice that when she was in the club, she would excuse herself by often saying, "*Hey. Give me a minute. I need to make a phone call*". 'Tracks' had a public telephone hanging-out area in the club. I was close to her, but still couldn't hear her side of the conversation.

During this period of "*I need space*", Renee introduced me to some friends from the New York area. All of us would hang out periodically - CJ included. It was awkward, but I went anyway. One of the women from the New York group caught my interest. She was very stunning - beautiful, to say the least. Her name was Marla. She was about six feet tall, had long legs, and a model-like size. She and I would hang back from the crowd of friends and just talk. Her friends would be watching her to see what her next move would be, as they didn't approve of her behavior. She came down to D.C. because she was in breakup-mode from her girlfriend back in Flushing, New York.

Scattered Pieces of the Puzzle

I could tell Marla was hurting and was in need of an outlet to take away her pain. We were kicking it at the club and having a great time. One night while at the club, she invited me to go to the car with her because she had left something behind. I accompanied her and, while in the car, we had a connection. Lust took over. We couldn't keep our hands off of each other. We had a heavy petting session right then and there - but no sex.

Marla's friends were livid! They couldn't believe her behavior and some words were said. Long story short, Marla and I kept in touch when she returned home to New York. We wrote letters back and forth to each other, and often spent countless hours on the phone until the wee hours of the morning.

One day, I was in my father's den writing a letter to her, but I didn't get to finish. It must be noted here that my mother **NEVER** goes into my father's office. Well, as I said, I didn't finish writing the letter. I hid it inside a billfold tablet and placed it in one of my father's drawers.

When I made it home from school, my sister called me on the phone. She asked, "*Are you standing up or sitting down?*" I told her I was standing. She said, "*Well you need to sit down.*" My stomach immediately took a dive.

"*What's wrong?*" I asked.

"*Do you know someone named Marla?*"

OH MY GOD! I knew right away what happened. I know I didn't leave anything out where anyone would be able to find and read the unfinished letter.

My sister continued. "*Mom found a letter you were writing to that woman. It took me* **hours** *to calm her down. She wants to talk to you.*"

My stomach did flips like one would flip a pancake on a griddle.

When I first came across mom after the revelation, she was tending to the children she cares for during the day. I kept skirting around not wanting to talk to her. I was **NOT** looking forward to this day.

I remember asking my godmother, "*What would you rather hear from me: I'm pregnant or I'm gay?*"

She replied, "*Neither.*"

Well, so much for that!

I was downstairs when I heard the dreaded sound of footsteps approaching. I could no longer run. I had to face the music and hear what she had to say.

The conversation took place in my godfather's den. She started crying immediately. I couldn't handle it. I almost lost my lunch because my stomach was so upset. I braced myself for the conversation that was about to take place.

Scattered Pieces of the Puzzle

I remember her first words very well:

"I failed you. What did I do wrong? Your father and I tried to raise you right, teach you good morals, and keep you in church." She then started placing blame on my friend, Shane. *"If he didn't take you around Reese and weren't exposed to what was going on with them, you would have never gone that way."*

Wait. A gay man made me gay? I rolled my eyes at that one.

"If I disappointed you, mom, I'm sorry. This was in me for a long time", I tried to explain.

She kept referring back to Shane and said it was he who introduced me to that lifestyle.

In response, I tried to explain it through the following analogy:

"It's like when I gave liver a try. I realized I didn't like it and didn't want to try it ever again. That's how I viewed relationships with men."

She insisted I was going through a phase and would soon "get over it".

I tried explaining to her that I was living the lifestyle for a year and that it wasn't a phase. The relationship between us was a little strained, but we seemed to be able to respect each other's space. We used to be able to talk about a lot of things, as I always felt comfortable talking to her about stuff. This 'situation' was the exception.

After my godmother found out about my relationship with Marla, things between Marla and I were tough to maintain. She invited me to visit, so I made the trip and met up with her and the others who had visited D.C. a few months back. We made **BIG** plans for my stay, but things didn't fall into place during the trip. Instead, we hung out for the weekend at clubs in the New York area.

CJ and I remained friends and occasionally talked to each other just to check in. It seemed like she was interested in maintaining a cordial friendship, and that was fine with me. I couldn't pine over something that was never really going to go anywhere.

Having my heart broken by a woman was much harder to deal with than when I broke up with boyfriends in the past. The hurt is so much deeper. Honestly, I was uncomfortable seeing CJ being single again. It took some time for my heart to heal.

Was that the road I had to look forward to? Having my heart shattered into a million pieces?

CHAPTER SEVEN
The Tightened Chain and More Scattered Pieces

I came to realize it takes time for one's heart to heal from relationships.

One day, the phone rang. On the other end was Marla. It was nice talking to her. We remained friends and eventually, her and her girlfriend got back together - during the course of her affair with me. She realized she wasn't quite over that girl.

The last Tuesday of the month was approaching, which meant that ladies' night at 'Tracks' was approaching as well. I figured it was time to go back out and 'fish' again. As I was walking through the club heading for the exit, I was approached by a shy, pretty young woman who stated she had ran into my friend Cat who I had met a year ago. She was with some new people. One lady she introduced me to had such a style and flair about herself. Her name was Vernell. Her smile could light up the room. This lady looked like she loves to have some fun!

I hung out with them for a while, just walking around the club. Cat and I got on the dance floor and cut a rug! Miss V was doing her thing, too. She had this thing she liked to do with her butt, and those studly women would eat it up. Cat would be laughing her heart out. They always came into the club lit up, drinking and smoking something other than cigarettes.

I set my sights on another young lady and proceeded to make my move. *"Hello. Are you with anyone?"*

"No, but I am here with a few friends. My name is Sora."

Sora had a mixed look about her. She extended her hand and I shook it as we introduced ourselves to each other. We moved to an area where we could talk and hear each other better. She had a southern hospitality flavor to her personality and invited me to meet up with her after her next set (she played the drums for a local band at another night spot in southeast D.C.). I was already impressed that she played the drums! Wow! I had a yearning to learn how to play drums when I was younger, but my mother said, *"That noise is **NOT** coming in this house!"* She made me take piano lessons instead.

That week seemed to move extremely fast. Friday night came and Sora invited me to her house. She was just getting in, and I helped her set up her drums. She was also an awesome cook. She browned some ground beef and added some cherry hot peppers over rice. Yummy! It was an easy and delicious little meal on the run. It was hard to find parking in the vicinity of her apartment - and the walls were too thin for my taste.

The Tightened Chain and More Scattered Pieces

The chemistry between Sora and me was different than what I experienced with CJ. I didn't know her well, but she had a way about her that was attractive and magnetic. She was originally from Georgia, which explained her southern flair. I wasn't sure where the relationship was going to go, and I didn't dare put all my eggs in one basket. I had to keep my heart close to my chest. I told her about my last relationship and how it ended. She kept saying, "*You are so pretty, Tanya*". All I could do was grin.

We talked a lot on the phone, getting to know each other. She wanted to know when she could see me again. Since she was willing to come over to my house, it would be sooner rather than later.

I had gotten a call earlier in the week from Carrie asking if I could drive her to school — about a three-hour drive away. I explained to Sora I had to take that trip and assured her Carrie and I were just friends — nothing more. I don't know **WHY** I felt the need to explain that to her. We weren't a couple, although I could really get into her.

I drove Carrie to school and helped her get settled in, as she had class the next day. She asked if I would be okay in the room by myself and I assured her I would be. She wanted to go out on campus and get into 'stuff'. I don't know why I agreed, but I did. While Carrie was away, I needed to comb my hair. I looked around her room for a comb or brush. When I opened a drawer, what did I see but the infamous diary she never allowed me to read. Well, my nosey self opened it and began to read.

My jaw started to drop and my eyes were like flaming darts. I was reading everything I suspected happened while we were in a relationship. I couldn't believe what I was reading! That b***h cheated on me - and she was graphic about each time!

I was literally sick to my stomach. The times I asked her if she was busy, she was actually out with Leslie. Then, when I introduced her to Renee, the same thing happened as well. I know we aren't together anymore, but it was interesting to learn she really thought she was the 'Player of the Year'. My friends were supposed to be my friends, but...

I was biting my lip hard, just waiting for her to get back to her room. I tried my best to not get too far ahead of what I just learned about her past.

When she returned to the dorm, she tried to get frisky with me. I didn't want her to touch me. She asked, *"What's wrong?"*

I blurted it out. *"I can't believe you cheated on me!"*

"What are you talking about?"

"I read your diary."

*"You did **WHAT**?"*

"You heard me."

The Tightened Chain and More Scattered Pieces

Well, that started a serious argument. Needless to stay, I couldn't stay there after all of that. I was fuming and driving away pissed off! I guess she got on the phone and consulted with her cheating coach, Anna. I didn't want anything more to do with Reese nor Leslie. I was **D.O.N.E.** It was time for a new chapter in my life.

Sora called, and I was happy to hear from her. Our relationship took off, with very little time to breathe. I spent time with her every day. Not a day went by when we didn't see each other. She spent the night over my house from time to time as well. I had a twin size bed, so when she spent the night, it was a tight squeeze. My godparents really liked her a lot. She was the "cat's meow". When she would stay the night, I would close the door. My godmother felt some type of way about having doors closed in her house. My godfather always knocked when I had company. I knew not to disrespect my parents' house, though.

Cat and Vernell approved of Sora as well. I told Sora, *"These ladies are my homies. We would occasionally hang out together - and they are a mess!"* I would pick up Ms. V and she would be cooking chicken while cussing out her three daughters (they were cute little girls).

One day, my dad said we can take his car and go on a vacation. We chose to drive to Williamsburg, Virginia. I never really discussed my sexuality with my godfather. I just assumed my godmother said something to him. He seemed to really take a liking to my new girlfriend.

That was actually the first time I felt comfortable saying Sora was my girlfriend.

One day, I walked into my bedroom and it was completely different. Sora was with me, and my godfather said, "*Hey! We bought a bigger bed for you and Tanya!*" My eyes bugged out! **What did he just say?** We laughed about that moment from time to time. Sora had gotten so comfortable with my parents, she started calling them mom and dad.

Sora needed to move out of her apartment to save money. I wasn't ready to move in with anyone. Fortunately, a lady from her job offered her a room in the house she had acquired from her ex-husband. Sora took her up on that offer. I often spent the night there. The 'landlord' shared with us that she once had a relationship with a woman. Wow. I suppose she was taking a break from being with women?

In its second year, the relationship between Sora and I changed. Something felt different. Sora began talking about her past and thing that happened to her. Our relationship did a downward spiral. I was again heartbroken. She started seeing some guy out of nowhere. I had such an insatiable jealousy streak that soon got the best of me.

When the guy would show up at her house, I found myself driving over there just to sit out front and watch. One day, I actually walked up to the door and rang the doorbell. She was shocked that I just "popped up". I made my way inside - with her protesting the entire time. The following hurt the most:

The Tightened Chain and More Scattered Pieces

I was introduced to that guy like I was just some woman off the street - and Sora and I had been together nonstop for two years! We looked at each other with a "knowing". Enough was said. I walked out and never returned.

I started hanging out on the regular with my friends Cat and Vernell. Whatever they did, I did. I would pick up Ms. Vernell and without fail, she would have a beer in her hand…and cooking chicken. This particular night, we were heading to the club. I needed and wanted to forget about everything that happened recently. Cat and Vernell were those kinds of friends who knew how to keep my mind off of those things that bothered me the most.

Day after day, they would check on me or we would go hang out. One day, there was a young woman standing at the bar who was absolutely stunning. Her beauty took my breath away. I noticed Vernell was talking to her like they knew each other. I asked, *"Who is **THAT**?"* She replied, *"Oh, girl. That's Dana. You want to meet her?"*

"Oh my God! She wouldn't want anyone like me. She appears to have a lot of class and professionalism about her."

Nonetheless, Vernell made the introduction. We hit it off pretty good! We exchanged numbers and kept in touch. One thing about Dana: she didn't drive. Any time we saw each other, I had to pick her up from either her house or job in downtown D.C. We got very comfortable with each other and planned little weekend getaways not too far from home.

One day, my phone rang. It was Sora calling. I was really salty with her and didn't have a whole lot to say. She wanted to know what I was up to. I gave her some smart, short remarks. One of her questions was, *"Are you seeing anyone?"* I didn't lie, but I kept our conversation close to the vest.

While out at the club in the middle of the afternoon one day, Dana and I were on the dance floor. I remember I was wearing a hoodie that day. I was having a great time, when out of the blue, someone pulled me off the floor by the hood. When I turned around, I was face-to-face with Sora. I was so embarrassed.

I asked her pointedly, *"How do you get any say-so in my life? You chose that man over me!"*

Sora sent flowers with apologies to my house, trying to smooth things over. I supposed she expected me to fall for her ploy. I really liked Dana, but I know she, too, was just getting out of a relationship and still had feelings for that person, just as I still had for Sora. Spending time with Dana kept me from thinking about the breakup and its ugly truth.

Over time, Dana and I talked things through. We both ended up back with the people who hurt us, but we did remain friends. My relationship with Sora picked back up, but something didn't feel right. That short break we had woke up something in me. Something in Sora's demeanor had changed. I couldn't quite put my finger on what was happening.

The Tightened Chain and More Scattered Pieces

Well, something happened that totally blew my mind. Sora was having an affair with her landlord! How did **THAT** happen? So now, the house I was always welcomed in had changed. I had to sneak around to see Sora. *What in the hell was wrong with me?*

I couldn't believe I had stooped down to that level of desperation. I even asked one of my brothers if I could use his place to have sex with Sora. Afterwards, I couldn't even drop her off in front of her house!

Finally, I snapped out of that 'love fog' and stopped sneaking around to see Sora. Obviously, what we had was completely over and it was time to move on with my life.

I went through a series of dating and sleeping with different women, including getting involved with an older woman I worked with. Come to find out, she lied to me about her age and had a horrible temper. That relationship ended abruptly. She used to get drunk and end up over at my apartment knocking on the door. My neighbors didn't know anything about my lifestyle, but with the way that woman carried on, I'm pretty sure they knew more than I gave them credit for. I finally let her in - a moment I lived to regret. She cornered me in my kitchen and held a knife to me. I knew she wasn't crazy enough to stab or kill me. When she snapped out of it, she lit a cigarette and begged me to come back to her. When I told her no, she took the lit cigarette and burned her two forefingers. I called a friend and left her in my apartment. It took my sister's boyfriend to get her out of my apartment the next day. It was time for me to leave that job. I left and started looking for another job.

My quest to find the perfect woman continued.

One day, I was at another club when I saw this woman who was checking out the scene. I just stared at her. She finally acknowledged me, came over, and spoke. She was pretty with a gap between her teeth. She said her name was Lilith. She seemed like she had it all together. As I got to know her, I detected a little arrogance about her.

Basically, she told me she was actually looking at someone else in the club that night, but I guess because the other woman wasn't interested, I was her second choice.

Okay, Lord. How do I keep meeting these crazy women?

This particular woman lived with her ex-fiancé, and they hung out together like they were the best of friends. I actually felt sorry for the guy. He obviously hadn't allowed himself to heal from their relationship.

Lilith used her sex appeal and knowing how to manipulate her way in the bedroom to get what she wanted from me. When she stayed over my house and I asked about help with cleaning the kitchen or any other chore, she used sex - sometimes with toys - to divert attention away from the requests. After a while, that living arrangement grew old.

The Tightened Chain and More Scattered Pieces

One night, when she wanted to use her sex payment plan, I gave her a stern **"NO!"** I stated several times I didn't want to do anything. She wouldn't take 'no' for an answer. She went into the bedroom, strapped on a toy, and forced herself on me. I felt so violated, all I could do was cry after she left. The word 'rape' entered my mind for the first time. *No one would ever believe I was raped by a woman with a strap-on.* I would have to take that secret to my grave.

The relationship with Lilith caused me so much mental and emotional pain. I ended up in the hospital one day thinking I had a heart attack from the stress. I couldn't contain my tears when my mother called me. I told her I was on my way to the hospital. She followed the ambulance to Prince George's Hospital.

Lilith worked at the hospital and was very surprised to see me there. My mother and sister were flaming mad because I allowed that woman's actions to send me to the hospital. At the time, I looked like one of those children from Cambodia that you see on TV. I was down to 110 pounds.

I lost complete and utter respect for Lilith. I wanted nothing else to do with her. I had taken and dealt with enough from her. Eventually, she quit the job at the hospital and moved away to Chicago with her ex-fiancé's niece.

I had to take some time to get myself together. The relationship with Lilith dragged my dignity through the mud. What was wrong with me? I allowed that woman to upset my entire world!

I remember having a beautiful sofa my sister-in-law's sister had given me. I let Lilith talk me into getting rid of it in order to replace it with an ugly futon that didn't match anything in my home. *Was it love or lust that made me do stupid stuff?*

My friend Cat decided it was time for a change of pace and moved away. Ms. Vernell stopped hanging out in the clubs, and we sort of lost contact with each other.

It was a difficult time in my life. My mom had passed away and my closest friends were going in different directions. I recall a conversation that took place before my birth mother passed away. She told me about a relationship she had with a woman named Amelia. I joked with her and asked, "*Is she the famous Amelia Earhart? You broke her heart and then she disappeared!*" She went on to explain the woman was aggressive and smothering. That was such a surprise to me. Perhaps homosexuality was hereditary…

I also used to talk to my mother about the birthmark on my forehead. One day, she kissed the spot on my forehead and said, "*You are a chosen one.*"

"*What? Chosen for **what**?*"

She and I used to have some really deep conversations. I remember trying my best to hide my sexuality from her, but it's almost like she always knew. When Sora and I were having difficulties, it was my mother's house I would end up over just to think.

The Tightened Chain and More Scattered Pieces

One particular day, my mother asked me, *"What's wrong?"*

"Nothing."

"Don't tell me nothing is wrong. You know that blood is thicker than water" (her famous line, **especially** when she was drinking).

"I had love problems."

Her reply shocked me because I was trying my best to keep my sexuality a secret from her. *"Was it a man problem or woman problem?"*

I was honest with her and stated it was a woman problem. She knew right away who it was and suggested I be weary of southern women.

Mom went on to say that that woman was going to break my heart - and she did. As I think about it, virtually everything that happened to me, mom had a sixth sense and would "know".

****

Well, whomever the Lord sends my way, I was **sure** she would have to be much better than Lilith. It was time to put myself in a new environment and perhaps go hang out with the young ladies I met at Hill Haven. They seemed nice enough.

We branched off to different places to hang out, meet new people, and network. The relationship that formed between us was awesome! Each of us got involved with different people and each of us experienced ups and downs in those relationships.

A new place opened up on the corner of Pennsylvania Avenue and 8th Street SE in West D.C. That place had a different feel to it with a different crowd. There was an eclectic feel and upscale touch. It was called "The Blue Penguin". The people who ran the place were inviting and gravitated towards their guests.

Indeed, that was the new place to be! There was a small pool table and an area where we could eat and mingle with the crowd. The grand opening was fabulous, with a different circuit of faces: Black, Spanish, and White women.

I had never been with a White woman before. It was something new and I was very inquisitive. I took notice of a young, White woman sitting at the bar with her guy friend. I was standing near her and she would glance my way and smile.

"Wow! Look at those piercing blue eyes and that red hair!" I thought. Her eyes drew me in right away.

The Tightened Chain and More Scattered Pieces

I sat and talked with her and her guy friend for quite a while. He seemed to be edging her on to speak and dance with me. We got up, hit the dance floor, and returned to our seats. A few drinks later, I found myself at her apartment in Virginia. I had **NEVER** done anything like that…going home with someone the first night we met. I usually waited at least four months before sleeping with someone. *What was it about this woman that changed my stance?*

She had an inviting smile and her eyes were like blue ice. I had never seen eyes as blue as hers. Her friend, Andy, seemed like he was there as support and was hoping he, too, would get lucky that night.

The next morning, I woke up at her house. I heard her talking to Andy about going to have a bit to eat at this place in Alexandria. She invited me to go along. She was a total different person when not under the influence of alcohol. The two of them chatted among each other a majority of the time. I decided to chime in on the conversation. She was dismissive. I couldn't even think of her name - until I heard Andy call her Leigha. It soon became apparent I was just a one-night stand.

I wasn't about to be someone's one-night stand. I had more integrity than that. Did I look like a unicorn? If that was what I was, then I guess it's too late now because I had slept with a woman I knew nothing about - not to mention the partners she had slept with in the past. Maybe that's what Leigha and Andy did: Go to clubs, meet people, and have one-night stands.

Well, Tanya: You screwed this up, didn't you?

I had stooped to a new low. I suppose I needed to shrug it off, call it a day, and forget it ever happened.

Ironically, I couldn't stop thinking about her. She gave me her number, and I decided to use it. We ended up talking for a while and made plans to meet up later. Maybe she felt bad, thinking I was going to be just another notch on her belt. We ended up going back to the club where we met.

Leigha seemed to have a different opinion of me then. We hit it off pretty well, despite the slow start. Our relationship took off fast. Before we both knew it, she asked if I would consider moving in with her.

Umm... Huh? *Did she just ask me to move in with her? I had never considered moving in with anyone.*

One thing I had to address was her smoking. I didn't realize she was a **HEAVY** smoker, and I really didn't care for people who smoked. I hated kissing an ashtray. She stated she would quit smoking before we moved in together.

We found a house to rent in northern Virginia. Two weeks before the move, she told me she wasn't going to stop smoking. I was mad as hell! Everything in me said, **"Don't move in with her!"** I felt like I had been tricked, especially since I had turned in my move-out notice to my apartment's leasing office.

The red flag was raised. I knew I wasn't going to be able to trust her. If she lied to me about that, what else would she lie about? My relationship with her was on edge.

The Tightened Chain and More Scattered Pieces

Leigha's family accepted me. I was even invited to her grandmother's cottage in the New England area. I received a lot of weird looks because it wasn't common for Blacks to be up in that neck of the woods. The family liked to party and throw back drinks. I couldn't deal with the drinking too much anymore. The strain on the relationship was apparent - and I wasn't sexually-attracted to her anymore.

I started hanging out in the AOL chat rooms talking to all types of people, especially young women and bisexual guys. One day, Leigha's suspicions got the best of her. While I was away at my pool league, she broke into my account to see who I was spending time talking to. When I returned, we got into a screaming match and she accused me of sleeping with the guy in the chat room.

After that, the relationship between she and I deteriorated. It was time to call it quits. She decided to move to Florida with her siblings. Some months down the line, she wanted to vacation together. I told her I wanted my own bed and that it was just two friends on vacation. She made reservations for Key West. We left from Fort Lauderdale, making our way to our destination. All the while, she was trying to get back together with me, but that soon took a turn. Apparently, she met someone there and was sleeping with her. Leigha wanted her affair to remain a secret, but the other girl let it slip out.

That sealed the deal for me. I knew there was **NO** reconnection possible on my part. I was done.

A few years down the line, I received a letter from her both apologizing and thanking me. She realized she had a drinking problem and decided to give it up and get clean.

After that relationship ended, I started hanging out with a new crowd. I was really trying to find my niche. It seemed I couldn't fit in anywhere.

I met a few people who liked country music and two-stepping - a cool style of dancing. I met a few interesting people, made friends…and had one brief affair.

*Here I go again. Why do I keep meeting these women who just **LOVE** to lie?*

Her name was Shadonna. She was a beautiful mixture of Mexican and Sicilian. She told me she was single, had a roommate, and two little boys. I could never get her to go out with me on a real date. Instead, she preferred coming to my house. One time, she did invite me over to meet the so-called "roommate".

There was another woman she hung out with who always gave me the evil eye whenever I came around. What did this woman have going on? The picture didn't add up right. The woman finally cornered me and told me that she and Shadonna had been seeing each other for a while. Apparently, they perform together in shows at a few clubs in the area.

The Tightened Chain and More Scattered Pieces

Shadonna saw that woman talking to me, and her eyes grew as big as saucers. The gig was up. I looked at the woman and then at Shadonna. Right then, I decided it was time to leave the drama. I got in my car and drove off. By the time I arrived at my house, I had a visitor waiting for me on my doorstep: Shadonna. She spewed out a laundry list of lies. By now, believe me: I know how to lie and how to recognize them.

Women get in a pinch, and the first thing out of their mouths are lies, lies, lies. Secretly, they hide their other relationships - and try to maintain one with others. Ludicrous!

I saw Shadonna for a couple more months and our relationship ended. Needless to say, it wasn't pleasant - but it was over.

I now know the meaning of the phrase, "*She fell off the turnip truck*" — only because I have fallen off plenty.

One day, I ran into a friend from my 1980s 'Tracks' days and her best friend. We started hanging out, and my friend took a liking to me. I soon learned we didn't live too far away from each other.

During this time, my life took another drastic turn. My godmother - the one who raised me - was ill and ended up in Prince George's Hospital. When I went to visit her, I knew she was never coming back home. A strong feeling rolled over me and, of course, I was correct. Roughly one week later, she passed away. I ended up moving back home with my godfather. Just over a year after my godmother's passing, he died. I moved out of my childhood home and in with a friend until I could get a new place of my own.

I started going to some WNBA (Women's National Basketball Association) games. One day after a game, my friends and I hung out at this spot not far from the Verizon Center. We were just sitting around and chit-chatting about the game - when what do I see? The most beautiful smile and eyes to match coming towards the table where we were sitting. When she approached, she asked, *"Can I join y'all? My name is Lia."* Everyone around the table introduced themselves.

I couldn't stop staring at her.

I told my friend who was seated next to me, *"Wow! She has some energy flowing and is so cute!"* (I never really considered dating a woman with dreadlocks before.)

I thought to myself, **"I would date her."**

The Tightened Chain and More Scattered Pieces

As the conversation continued to flow around the table, Lia heard me mention Country and Western music and two-stepping. Those words immediately grabbed her attention. Later, we exchanged numbers and set up to meet when she returned from a trip to Africa. I found it intriguing that she traveled a few times a month to various destinations in the Motherland.

Something was totally different about Lia. I had never met anyone like her. I did hear her mention she was bisexual, and my antennae went way up. I didn't want to date anyone who was bisexual. In her words: "*I'm not dating at the moment and not really interested in men right now. I'm monogamous.*" I could tell she was sincere.

The manner in which she spoke sort of intimidated me. She was fluent in several languages. "*I'm not in this woman's league*", I thought to myself. Nonetheless, we enjoyed each other's company. She didn't own a car, but she managed to get around town with one of those car-sharing programs called 'Zipcar'.

Lia invited herself over to my apartment in Arlington, Virginia. She had this affectionate way about herself. I just wanted to cozy up to her. She was very tiny in stature and the perfect size for cuddling.

She owned a house with her roommate, Erin. The seemed to have shared a lot together, having gone in to buy a home. That was one heck of a friend!

Lia and I enjoyed the various dimensions of our relationship. I had grown extremely comfortable with my sexuality by then. She liked to kiss in public, but I had a problem with that. I didn't want people to look and judge. She would always say, "*No one's watching. It's your imagination.*" I would sneak and give her a kiss - and then shrink up. Our relationship was so smooth, it was almost scary. We did everything together. She was very active, which brought out the competitive side from each other with activities such as bowling, tennis, and even bike riding.

We started a bike club for more of our friends to join us on Saturday or Sunday mornings. We also discovered our backgrounds related to our faith were similar, in that we both grew up in the church. A few times, we discussed finding a church home - a place where we felt comfortable attending as a gay couple. We found a church to attend in the D.C. area that suited that need and desire.

The relationship with Lia lasted a few years. I was always on the lookout, waiting for the other shoe to drop and for her to disappointment - a product of my short-term relationships from my past. The relationship with her was refreshing. The time came for me to meet a few of her relatives and friends. To make the introduction as fun as possible, a cruise with her family was planned. We had an awesome time.

The Tightened Chain and More Scattered Pieces

I truly loved Lia. She was so supportive of my activities. I believe the reason our relationship was not like the others was because we were both mature and could distinguish between what was important…and not so important. Discovering we were both "people persons" helped a lot, too. No matter the background of person, we interacted with them and enjoyed the variety life had to offer.

Her biological parents were also deceased, and she had very little family that was spread throughout the country.

I was very much in love with Lia. I just knew she was the right woman for me. I was so confident in our love and commitment, I gave her a promise ring on Valentine's Day. I presented it to her over dinner, with the waitress as our audience in the background. I didn't receive the reaction to my gesture and profession of love that I wanted. It was yet another failed Valentine's Day…

Lia's career was taking a slight detour. She was stepping out into the field of becoming a Consultant. One project she was working towards was filled with uncertainty. She was getting depressed from not working. She finally had something that was going to take her out of the country for something more than her usual travels to Africa.

What was this going to mean for our relationship?

While she was away, we used Skype almost every day to communicate. She was scheduled to be away for at least two months. She returned in October and was home for the holidays. We definitely made the most of our time together.

Still...

Something seemed a little different. I couldn't quite put my finger on it.

We discussed me visiting her in Africa. I had never been and thought it would be a great opportunity to take a vacation and cultivate our relationship. I was so excited about the trip. I was saving my vacation days from work and money. I knew the trip was going to be quite pricey. I also had to schedule the shots necessary to protect me from the elements of disease that were running rampant in those third world countries.

After her time back home, Lia returned to Liberia doing more of what she was tasked to do. We continued our regular conversations and I grew more and more excited about my upcoming trip. As the time for me to join her neared, her voice and conversations began to sound different. I asked her if everything was okay, and she stated everything was fine. I had a sense of unease with her response.

I also asked if she wanted me to bring any of our sex toys, and she replied, "*If you want*". That lackadaisical response had an undertone of uncertainty. I kept talking.

She then dropped something on me that scared me to the core: "*Don't get wrapped up in what I'm doing.*"

That part of the conversation seemed to come out of nowhere. That was not something that sounded pleasant to the ears of someone who was prepared to visit. She went on:

The Tightened Chain and More Scattered Pieces

"Maybe this isn't a good time for you to come."

*"**WHAT?** I have less than two weeks! It's the perfect time to regain our relationship and get closer. I made the necessary calls and everything was in place for my visit!"*

Note: I had no idea all that was planned to prepare for a trip outside of the U.S. It was a lot—and those shots were no walk in the park.

So, there I was: Two weeks before the trip, and Lia started saying things that didn't make any sense to me. It was almost like she was trying to talk me out of coming to Liberia. *"This is a fine time to tell me this, Lia. What is the issue?"* She didn't say.

How was I going to get my money back at that late date for the trip? I had spent $2,500 for the airline tickets, shots, and medications I would need. I also hoped I had accrued enough time for leave from the job.

When we hung up our call, my spirit wasn't settled. I was left to wonder: *Was it me or is she really changing her mind? Maybe her workload is wearing her down.* I **hoped** that was *ALL* that was happening…

On the day of the trip, May 2, 2006, I knew it was going to be a long flight - a day and a half of travel. I was leaving from Dulles International Airport, flying into Brussels, one hour in Senegal, and then to Monrovia. When I arrived at my final destination, I watched and took notes on all of the craziness going on around me. People were being shaken down for money because they didn't have the right type of papers or whatever else the 'shakers' could get away with. This was happening in the customs area. The officer there was checking everyone's bags as they came through.

I happened to catch sight of a sign in Monrovia that read:

"If you are caught with anything morally against this country, the penalty is jail time."

My stomach hit the ground. I had a bag **FULL** of sex toys! All I could think of was how would I get out of that? When the officer made it to me, he asked, *"What is your business here?"*, I immediately said, *"ABA* [American Bar Association]: *Congo Town"*. He backed away from me with his hands in the air and said, *"You can go"*. He never even checked my bag.

My cellphone didn't work there. How in the world would I have been able to call Lia to tell her I was arrested for bringing sex toys into the country? I couldn't even begin to imagine having to explain that to my family or friends. Thank God; I didn't have to go through any of that.

The Tightened Chain and More Scattered Pieces

Lia and her driver were on the other side of the door waiting for me when I exited. YES! I made it to Liberia, Africa to see my sweetheart! I hoped for a very nice trip, especially because I had always wanted to visit Africa *(I would've preferred the animal kingdom, though...some place like Tanzania)*. Well, that wasn't where she was working, so Liberia it was. I was just glad I finally had a reason and chance to visit the country.

When Lia and I finally seen each other, she grabbed me, hugged me, and squeezed me tightly. She introduced me to her driver, John. I could hardly understand him. He spoke with a mixture of Liberian and English. Lia translated some of his words for me.

We drove for approximately 30 minutes, driving past places that looked abandoned. I recall seeing an amputee soccer team at play. They were all running on one leg, almost better than those players with two! We finally made it to her place and unpacked the bags. Then, she introduced me to some of the people she talked about - and her dog.

What I really wanted was another nice, long hug and a few kisses. She hugged me, but buffed my kisses. *Hmm... That was not like her.* She was a very affectionate person. When it came to sex, we had quite a bit of chemistry.

I didn't want to focus too much on what happened. Maybe she was tired and thinks I'm tired, too. After a good night's rest, I would see what tomorrow will bring.

The next morning, I woke up feeling frisky. I scooted over to her. She shoos me off, gets out of the bed, and head into the bathroom. I walked up behind her and hugged her from the back. Again, she shooed me away.

What is this resistance? I had never experienced anything like that from her.

Lia grabbed me by the hand and led me back to the bedroom. Right away, my stomach fell into my lap. She told me to have a seat and then begins to explain…very slowly. She started talking about a guy she met and explained that she can't be openly gay in this country, blah, blah, blah. Apparently, the man she met was a dignitary from that country, and she was attracted to him.

PLEASE! SOMEBODY SLAP ME! I must be having a nightmare. Surely, the woman I've been chatting with on a regular basis didn't just tell me she is interested in some man from another **CONTINENT**! The anger began to rise up in me. In that moment, I wanted to slap her into the middle of next week…**TWICE!**

I started asking 1,000 questions, beginning with:

HOW DID THAT HAPPEN?

She did her best to answer all of my questions. I stopped her and said, "*Wait. That means the first time you came back home for the Christmas holiday, you had already met him?*"

The Tightened Chain and More Scattered Pieces

Her response was silly to me. "*I didn't say I was in love with him. It's more like hero worship.*"

My whole world seemed to be crumbling down around me. I couldn't believe I flew over 8,000 miles across the **WORLD** to have my heart broken into a million pieces. I was stuck. I had to endure the pain for three whole weeks because I couldn't find an early flight back home. How was the rest of the trip going to fair?

Dear God,
You have to help me get through this one.

I have **NEVER** had something as traumatic as that happen to me — especially the way it happened.

May 25th could not come fast enough for me. For the remainder of my stay, I was placed in the hands of her driver. Lia and I kept things very close to the vest. I had to hide my emotions, and it was **HARD**.

There was a time I was able to get on the internet while there to send an email. I sent a note to my pastor back in D.C. explaining what happened. She knew Lia and I were a couple - and she also knew I was away on a trip to see her.

My pastor was quite surprised to receive an email from me telling her all that I had been going through. For me, it was devastating, having to walk around with my heart literally bleeding. She gave me some good advice and suggested I make the most of the trip. She left me with the following encouraging quote:

Tanya S. Meade

"Just because it's a bend in the road does not mean it's the end of the road — unless you fail to make the turn."

Somehow, I managed to embrace and hold on to that quote. It actually made the remainder of my trip a tad bit easier. When I left, the sex toys I had brought along stayed behind with her. I know beyond a shadow of a doubt that it was God who kept me from losing my mind and whipping her butt. After all, I couldn't afford to end up in a foreign jail.

Returning home was another sad moment in time. I cried all the way to Brussels. I had a lot to think about. I still had questions, with the primary one being: What type of person would do what was done to me? **A selfish one.** That's who. Lia should have told me something back in October - the time when I heard and felt the change in the atmosphere of our relationship. With tears still streaming down my face, the memories of my trip to Africa lay in ruins.

The flood of embarrassment came over me. So many people who knew us as a couple also knew I was going overseas for a special visit to see Lia. Now, I had to go back and tell everyone the trip wasn't at all what I expected it to be.

After traveling almost two days and finally back on American soil, reality crept in. Lia and I were no longer a couple. The longest intimate relationship of my life was really over.

The Tightened Chain and More Scattered Pieces

A few friends gathered around me to let me vent and heal my way through the process. It was actually made easier because she wasn't anywhere around and I didn't have to run into her at every turn. My mind wandered into a dark place - one where I imagined her and 'that man' together. I honestly don't know if she slept with him, but I told myself that she did. That thought enabled me to get past the situation faster.

I could only take each day as it came. I began spending more time on the internet. I came upon this site where I could talk to celebrities from other countries and ended up meeting all kinds of people. In its own way, it was a lot like today's social media outlets. I found myself talking to an actress' fans on an exotic site and began ordering various types of X-rated DVDs. The ones I ordered had a storyline *(as if that fact was going to change the films' contents)*. Ha!

Anyway, the site was like a social network. Those people became my friends—although I didn't know them from Adam. Still, we all had something in common: We were lonely people needing love and attention in any way we could get it. I was even invited to Budapest to attend one of their film award ceremonies. I really wanted to go, but I didn't want to spend the money. Plus, I had no idea about what dangers lie ahead with those strangers.

The porn DVDs got old really quick. I needed another outlet. I heard somewhere that Guiding Light (the soap opera) had a lesbian storyline going on. Soon enough, I found myself hooked on the show. There was actually an online discussion group set up for the show on that topic. Again, I met a new set of people who helped take my loneliness away. I was all over the place and into all kinds of things, all in an effort to find my footing again. My tickets to the WNBA games became a regular and fun outing for me.

One day, I joined a Facebook group and started building a network of acquaintances and friends. I was doing all I could to keep my mind off of the failed relationship. Out of the blue, a young woman by the name of Missy messaged me. She said she was checking out my page, so I checked out hers as well. She asked if I was going to the upcoming basketball game, and I told her I would be there. This conversation happened about midweek. She then stated she wanted to meet up after the game. I wasn't feeling it. I suggested we meet another time.

As it turned out, King's Dominion was hosting its annual event for the LBGTQ community. We decided that was the perfect time to meet. Up until that day, we talked almost every day by either Facebook chat or phone. That was a change of pace for me — and a breath of fresh air. I needed the distraction.

The Tightened Chain and More Scattered Pieces

Missy and I began to get to know one another and spent some time together. Questions about each other's past were raised. On my part, I was 100% honest and told her, *"Before I get involved with anyone else, I needed to get over my past relationship"*. She said she was going through the same thing. There were times when she would talk about her ex, and I would see her light up with joy and be pissed off at the same time.

I **wanted** to believe she was truly over that other woman.

I **wanted** to trust that she was being honest. Call it my sixth sense or woman's intuition, something didn't seem right.

During this time, Lia came back into the picture. Unlike Missy, I did the noble thing and told my Lia the feelings I had for her were long gone. I didn't let her travel over 8,000 miles to find me with a broken heart. She was saddened by the news, but I'm glad I was honest. It probably would have been easier to tell a lie, but I didn't feel the need to.

Well, the relationship with Missy was a lot like a rollercoaster ride—and not in a good way. She introduced me to strip bars. It wasn't really my 'thing', but I was trying my best to fit in to her world. Our relationship lasted longer than it should have, only because I kept trying to give her a chance to change. The longer I stayed, the situation worsened. The lies she told became her staple form of speech. I think she actually believed her own lies!

I felt like my world was spinning out of control again. I needed to change a whole lot of who I was. I started attending church regularly and got involved in church activities. I wanted a deeper relationship with God, but I didn't know how to get there. At this point, I had been attending the same church for almost 10 years.

The relationship that Lia and I had was over, but we remained friends. Whenever she would come into town, I would make time to see her.

Missy would be up to her tricks. Her mouth would say one thing, but her actions said something else. I finally reached my fed-up point with her. Deep down inside, we both knew our relationship was over - even before it got started.

Note: When you enter a relationship and are *still* holding onto hurt, pain, resentment, and bitterness, it's hard to maintain a decent relationship with someone new.

In time, Missy met someone new. She acknowledged she was in love with the new woman and had finally let go of the hurts of her past. I was genuinely happy for her, despite our "ugly end".

That's just who I am; someone who chooses to move on with life because life it truly too short to dwell on negativity. My life's focus turned to going to church and seeking out where God wanted me to go.

The Tightened Chain and More Scattered Pieces

I had a friend named Kay who would call me occasionally. She had a great listening ear. I thought she was nice enough and had all the traits necessary to have a good relationship, but there was a problem: I wasn't physically attracted to her. She kept trying to tell me that she always inquired about me through other people. Me? I rarely inquired about her. I was still (in my own way) selfish.

I tried to see if I could fall in love with her or even catch some feelings for her with the way she felt about me. We dated for about six months. She simple wasn't who or what I wanted. I couldn't **MAKE** myself feel something that wasn't there. Eventually, I had to tell her the truth. She was not the least bit happy. She tried everything to persuade me to stay, including throwing my past up in my face:

"How was it that you could let your last ex do all of those crazy things to you, and you still be in love with her? Why won't you give me a chance?"

Kay tried everything, but my feelings for her could not extend past that of a friendship. She was a beautiful, professional woman who loved the Lord. Who wouldn't want those qualities? In an imperfect world, she would have been an awesome choice of a mate.

If only I had the ability to turn my feelings on and off like a light switch…

As I moved into the deeper things of Christ, I became more involved in the new church I joined. I was on a committee to help the community around the church. We tried to have planning meetings. Well, one of the young women on the committee was in charge of passing out the flyers. I wasn't available to get together on the day we had planned.

That Sunday, she asked if I would be interested in going to brunch or lunch with her after church. Talking to her, I could feel some of the pain she felt. We seemed to connect on a spiritual-attraction level. I wasn't sure where this was going. I really wasn't looking for a relationship. I knew right away that things were going to be done 100% differently with her.

I had it all planned out. I would not sleep with her for about four or five months down the line. Our relationship was going to be based on our spiritual walk. She had to love the Lord more than me. Well, I found out a lot while dating that woman, including the fact that she wasn't an animal-lover.

Our relationship turned dicey because she wanted me to give up my cats. I stayed at her house more often than she was at mine. She wanted to be able to spend time with me at my home. I was pretty much bending over backwards to please her, such as replacing my carpeting with new flooring. I made investments in all types of products to remove the cat hair from the floor and pieces of clothing. She had a series of issues, to the point that I knew the relationship wasn't going to last much longer.

The Tightened Chain and More Scattered Pieces

No way was I going to give away my pets and then the relationship with her doesn't work out. I would be out of pets **AND** a girlfriend. I could only be myself, and I wasn't going to budge where my pets were concerned. Sure enough, we ended up breaking up—and then got back together. **Why did I do that?** The problem **never** got resolved.

I ended up becoming an ordained deacon at the church. People would say to me, "*You won't be a deacon for long.*" I refused to receive those words. I was going before the Lord. I believed that was where He wanted me - as a leader in that church.

The church was looking for a way to broadcast the services, so we began recording on Facebook. I branched off and started checking out Periscope. I thought I would see what other available media outlets were available. On Periscope, I saw this man named Prophet Marcus who was teaching how to worship. From there, I was drawn to watch other scopes.

One day, I saw this woman named Sophia Ruffin. She was talking about how she got delivered from homosexuality. I turned her off and found a different scope. I felt some type of way. I wasn't sure what was happening. It was almost like a magnet was pulling me over there. I would attend Bible study at church and tell some of my friends about Periscope. They all signed up and got the app on their phones.

I found myself on Periscope all of the time. I listened to some really good teachings and shared them on Facebook. One day, I felt the need to do my own scope and tell others what God was doing in my life.

I began talking to the Lord about Sophia Ruffin. She had written a book called From Point Guard to Prophet. I was interested in the Prophetics, but I didn't know why. I said to the Lord, "*I have been in this gay life for 32 years. None of the relationships worked out for me. What's going on? I see this woman who used to look like a stud* [Sophia Ruffin] *who now looks like a blooming rose.*"

I thought to myself, "*If she got delivered from homosexuality, maybe there **IS** something wrong with being gay.*"

CONCLUSION

I was awakened three nights in a row and kept hearing "Romans 1" in my sleep. I was like, "*What is going on?*" Finally, after the third night, I opened up the Bible to Romans 1:26-28:

"For the cause God gave them up unto vile affections: for even their women did change the natural use into that which is against nature. And likewise also the men, leaving the natural use of the woman, burned in their lust toward another; men with men working that which is unseemly, and receiving in themselves that recompense of their error which was meet. And even as they did not like to retain God in their knowledge, God gave them over to a reprobate mind, to do those things which are not convenient."

It hit me like a ton of bricks. It was like God was calling me from the homosexual lifestyle. I profusely went through the Bible reading what the Lord gave me to read. I also Googled many passages of scripture looking for same-gender loving couples in the Bible. I realized one thing almost immediately:

THERE WERE NONE!

God reminded me that when He created man, He put Adam to sleep and pulled a woman from his rib. I realized my life as it was did not line up with the Word of God. **Nowhere** within the pages of the Holy Bible were there any gay *couples*. It has been preached in some of the LBGTQ churches that David and Jonathan were more than "covenant brothers"; however, I was led to several scriptures about homosexuality and how I was operating in "error". It was something that was a necessity after sitting under the teachings of other pastors who painted a rosy picture of living a homosexual lifestyle that was *completely opposite* of God's Word.

Here are a just a few of the scriptures that completely knocked my socks **OFF**!

"If a man lies with a male as if he were a woman, both men have committed an offense (something perverse, unnatural, abhorrent, and detestable); they shall surely be put to death; their blood shall be upon them"
(Leviticus 20:13, ESV).

"Or do you not know that the unrighteous will not inherit the kingdom of God? Do not be deceived: neither the sexually immoral, nor idolaters, nor adulterers, nor men who practice homosexuality"
(1 Corinthians 6:9, ESV).

"Just as Sodom and Gomorrah and the surrounding cities, which likewise indulged in sexual immorality and pursued unnatural desire, serve as an example by undergoing a punishment of eternal fire"
(Jude verse 7, ESV).

Conclusion

The next week, I was getting ready for Bible study and I was worshipping God. It actually started on my way home in the car. I went upstairs and found myself on my face, crying uncontrollably and thanking God. I was crawling around on the floor. *What was happening to me?* I went on to Bible study that night and felt so different. Something had happened to me while on that floor.

I found it very hard to concentrate on anything the pastor was saying. The next Sunday, as one of the elders was preaching, I didn't feel the anointing like I had before. It took everything I had in me to hone in on the message. Nothing felt the same.

God began to tell me it was time for me to leave that church. Fear enveloped me. I was, after all, a leader in the church.

I was obedient to God's prompting. I intended share God's direction with the pastor, resign from the position, and leave that church. I ended up inboxing a lady from Periscope named Corazon who talked about her daughter being gay, and she prayed for me. I told her I was leaving the church and needed some encouragement.

The day came for me to turn in my resignation letter and robe. It was almost like the pastor had been expecting me to do that. God showed up before me and paved the way for a smooth transition. I left that church and never looked back. God started closing the doors to that part of my life.

God also led me to call my friend of 32 years—one of the women I used to party with. She is now a **GREAT** Evangelist, Prophet, Pastor, and Teacher of the Gospel of Jesus Christ. I called her a week after formally resigning from the church, and she gave me downloads from Heaven concerning the prophecy the Lord had spoken to her about me. I was completely blown away.

She also gave me a book titled *The Divine Revelation of Hell* by Mary Baxter **(a HIGHLY-recommended read)**. I read the book from cover to cover, and by the time I was finished, I was "scared to death"! I knew this one thing for sure: I did **NOT** want to end up in Hell.

The book was a true story written by a woman whom God took to Hell for 30 days. Written on the pages of the book, Mary wrote that Hell was shaped like a human body. She also mentioned there was a section in the **ETERNAL LAKE OF FIRE** *just* for homosexuals.

God spoke to me and said, "*Hell isn't just about the fire and the devil; it's about the absence of **ME** from your life...**FOREVER**.*"

Today, I am 53 years old and have lived a homosexual lifestyle for 32 years. God told me there are many who need to know my story. There are many that need to know He is a God of miracles, signs, and wonders. You, too, can live a life of **PEACE** and abundant **JOY** that comes directly from our Heavenly Father.

Conclusion

Ephesians 4:7 speaks of a peace that surpasses **ALL** understanding. I get it now. I *know* that peace. I have never felt an anointing on my life such as I have now—**NEVER**. The blessings from God are just pouring in!

There's one more passage of scripture I'd like to share with you before I go. It's very encouraging and comes from Malachi 3:10. It reads:

" *Bring the full tithe into the storehouse, that there may be food in my house. And thereby put me to the test, says the Lord of hosts, if I will not open the windows of heaven for you and pour down for you a blessing until there is no more need.*"

All of the aforementioned passages of scripture used to be very vague or completely overlooked by me. I never grasped the full value of them…until now.

I'm finally free!

There are no more chains holding me!

That is why it was so important for me to write this book. I went through the mess and God made it a message. My test turned into a **TESTIMONY!** To God be the **GLORY!**

When He knocked on my heart, I was ready to say "**YES, LORD!**"

God took the Pieces of my Heart and gave me Peace.

"Thou shalt tread upon the lion and adder: the young lion and the dragon shalt thou trample under feet."

"Because he hath set his love upon me, therefore will I deliver him: I will set him on high, because he hath known my name.

He shall call upon me, and I will answer him: I will be with him in trouble; I will deliver him, and honour him.

With long life will I satisfy him, and shew him my salvation."

Psalm 91:13-16 (KJV)

ABOUT THE AUTHOR

Tanya S. Meade was born and raised in Seat Pleasant, Maryland - a small town famous for sporting and other recreational activities in the 1970s. She was actively engaged in a host of activities in her youth, to include being a member of the Girl Scouts, bowling, softball, and swimming. A significant aspect of her rearing that she transparently and unashamedly shares is her being birthed by one mother, yet raised by another. As a member of Mt. Pleasant Baptist Church in Washington, D.C., her Godmother ensured her foundation was rooted in Christianity through church attendance, singing in the choir, and a position held as a Junior Church Clerk.

With a desire to become a Registered Nurse, Tanya attended the University of the District of Columbia in the 1980s. Soon after, she had a change of heart and career path. In 1988, she was introduced to a woman who was seeking to employ a Histology Tech. Today, Tanya is diligently serving in two prominent positions: as a Histology Tech for more than 27 years at various hospitals in the D.C. area, and as a Pathology Researcher at Howard University Hospital.

Tanya S. Meade

Tanya is also a licensed Minister and awaiting ordination as an Evangelist. The Lord spoke the following to her: "*You will be in ministry full time, with more books to come.*" Her next piece of literary art will address living a holy life after coming out of homosexuality, while encouraging the reader to remain upright and righteous before the Lord.

Tanya is available for speaking engagements at your event or for your organization. Contact her at:
PiecesToPeaceMinistries@gmail.com

****

*"I went down to the bottoms **and** the very roots of the mountains; the earth with its bars closed behind me forever. Yet You have brought up my life from the pit **and** corruption, O Lord my God. When my soul fainted upon me [crushing me], I earnestly and seriously remembered the Lord; and my prayer came to You, into Your holy temple."*
Jonah 2:6-7 (AMP)

www.ingramcontent.com/pod-product-compliance
Lightning Source LLC
Chambersburg PA
CBHW071527080526
44588CB00011B/1586